Artificial Fireworks: Improved To The Modern Practice

With all ingrediants, compositions, preparations, moulds and manner to make fireworks; refining salt-petre and how to extract it

by Captain Robert Jones

with an introduction by Roger Chambers

This work contains material that was originally published in 1776.

This publication was created and published for the public benefit, utilizing public funding and is within the Public Domain.

This edition is reprinted for educational purposes and in accordance with all applicable Federal Laws.

DISCLAIMER

This book was written in an age when the home manufacture of fireworks was widely acceptable throughout society. In many places throughout the world, this is now a heavily regulated practice.

The material presented herein is intended to be strictly for educational purposes with the purpose of enlightening those interested in fireworks about their historical production. Publication of the material is neither an endorsement, nor a criticism of its contents. This book is presented as part of large series of educational historical material.

As the reader, please consider it your duty to become familiar with local, state, provincial and federal laws relating to the subject matter contained herein before attempting to utilize any of the information presented.

As the author, publisher and retailer cannot control how the reader utilizes the historical information presented in the pages herein, they hereby disclaim any liability to any party for any loss, damage, disruption or other liability that may be incurred by the reader's misuse of this material.

Self Reliance Books

Get more historic titles on animal and stock breeding, gardening and old fashioned skills by visiting us at:

http://selfreliancebooks.blogspot.com/

Introduction

I am pleased to present yet another title in our "How To ..." series.

The work is in the Public Domain and is re-printed here in accordance with Federal Laws.

As with all reprinted books of this age that are intended to perfectly reproduce the original edition, considerable pains and effort had to be undertaken to correct fading and sometimes outright damage to existing proofs of this title. At times, this task is quite monumental, requiring an almost total "rebuilding" of some pages from digital proofs of multiple copies. Despite this, imperfections still sometimes exist in the final proof and may detract from the visual appearance of the text.

I hope you enjoy reading this book as much as I enjoyed making it available to readers again.

Roger Chambers

CONTENTS.

CONTENTS.

Swans

CONTENTS.

Printed for and Sold by J. MILLAN.

1 LIST of his Majesty's Land Forces and Marines, at Home and Abroad, on Full and Half Pay, for 1776; also Lists of the Army from 1754, or any Year separate.

2 Muller's Works of Fortification, Engineering, Mining, &c. 8 vol. 2l. 8s. 6d.

3 Simes's Military Guide, containing a System of the Art of War, Parade and Field Duty, Regulations, Orders, Returns, Warrants, Salutes, &c. above 100 Figures on Copper.

4 Simes's Military Medley and Dictionary.

5 Discipline for the Norfolk Militia, by Lord Townshend, &c. sewed, 10s. 6d.

6 Major Young's Manœuvres, and new System of Fortification, Wolfe's Orders, &c. 10s. 6d.

7 New Exercise by his Majesty's Order, 1s.

8 Recruiting Book for the Army, 2s. 6d.

9 Regimental Book beautifully engraved, 4l. 4s.

10 Returns for Horse, Dragoons, and Foot, Attestations, Furloughs, Discharges, &c.

11 New Prussian Field Regulations, Cuts, 7s. 6d.

12 Captain Miller's Art of Self-Defence, on Copper Plates.

12 Vegetius's ancient Art of War, with Notes by Captain Clarke, 5s.

13 List of the Forces of above 40 Sovereigns, &c. neatly coloured, 10s. 6d.

14 Value of Commissions on Full and Half Pay, 2s.

15 New Art of War, by Captain Anderson, 7s. 6d.

16 Marine Volunteer, by Ologhlin, Cuts.

17 Plans and Forts of America, from actual Surveys.

18 Jones's Artificial Fireworks, with the Addition of Fireworks, Ordnance, &c. on a new Construction, for Sea and Land Service. by Mr. Muller.

19 Drummer's Instructor, with the English and Scotch Duty, Beatings, Marchings, Calls, &c. by R. Spencer, 2s.

20 Bland's Military Discipline.

21 Major Rogers's Journal of the late War in America, 5s.

22 Major Rogers's concise Account of America, also the interior Parts, their many Nations and Tribes of Indians on the great Lakes and Rivers, their Customs, Government, Number, &c. with many useful and entertaining Facts never before thought of, 5s.

23 Ponteach, or the Savages of America, a Tragedy, 1s. 6d.

24 Dillenius's General History of Land and Water Mosses, Corals, &c. 1l. 11s. 6d.

25 The History, Analysis, &c. of above 200 very rare flowering Plants, Flowers, Parts of Flowers, Flies, &c. drawn and engraved on 19 Folio Plates, by the late ingenious George Ehret, F.R.S. &c. beautifully coloured from his original Drawings, 1l. 11s. 6d.

26 Sheldrake's Herbal on above 100 large Folio Copper Plates, drawn in the most masterly Manner from the Originals, when in their highest Perfection, 4l. 4s.—6l. 6s. Royal.

27 Sheldrake on Heat and Cold for Greenhouses, 1s.

28 Columella on Agriculture, by Gitson, 4to. 15s.

ARTIFICIAL

FIREWORKS.

Sect. I.—Saltpetre.

SALTPETRE being the principal ingredient in fire-works, and a volatile body, by reason of its aqueous and aërial parts, is easily rarified by fire ; but not so soon when foul and grofs, as when purified from its crude and earthy parts, which greatly retard its velocity : therefore, when any quantity of Fireworks are to be made, it should be examined ; for if it is not well cleanfed, and of a good fort, your works will not have their proper effect; neither will it agree with the standing proportions of compofitions : but to prevent accidents I shall proceed with the method of refining it.

To refine Saltpetre.

Put into a copper, or any other veffel, 100 lb. of rough nitre with 14 gallons of clean water; let it boil gently half an hour ; as it boils take off the scum; then stir it, and before it settles put it into your filtering bags, which must be hung on a rack, with glazed earthen pans under them, in which must be sticks laid acrofs for the cryftals to adhere to ; it must stand in the pans 2 or 3 days to shoot, then take out the cryftals and let them dry : the water that remains in the pans boil again an hour, and strain it into the pans as before, and the faltpetre will be quite clear and tranfparent;

B

if not, it wants more refining, to do which proceed as usual, till it is well cleansed of all its earthy parts.

N. B. Those who do not chuse to procure their saltpetre by the above method, may buy it ready done, which for fireworks in general will do.

To pulverise SALTPETRE.

Take a copper kettle whose bottom must be spherical, and put into it 14 lb. of refined saltpetre, with 2 quarts or 5 pints of clean water; then put the kettle on a flow fire, and when the saltpetre is dissolved, if any impurities arise, skim them off, and keep constantly stirring it with 2 large spatulas, till all the water exhales; and when done enough, it will appear like white sand, and as fine as flour; but if it should boil too fast, take the kettle off the fire, and set it on some wet sand, which will prevent the nitre from sticking to the kettle. When you have pulverised a quantity of saltpetre, be careful to keep it in a dry place.

To extract SALTPETRE from damaged GUN-POWDER.

Have some filtering bags, hung on a rack, with glazed earthen pans under them, in the same manner as those for refining saltpetre: then take any quantity of damaged powder, and put it into a copper, with as much clean water as will cover it; when it begins to boil take off the scum, and after it has boiled a few minutes, stir it up; then take it out of the copper with a small hand kettle for that purpose, and put some into each bag, beginning at one end of the rack, so that by the time you have got to the last bag, the first will be ready for more; continue thus, till all the bags are full; then take the liquor out of the pans, which boil and filter, as before, 2 or 3 times, till the water runs quite clear, which you must let stand in the pans some time,

and

and the faltpetre will appear at top. To get the faltpetre entirely out of the powder, take the water from that already extracted, to which add fome fresh and the dregs of the powder that remain in the bags, and put them in a veffel, to ftand as long as you pleafe, and when you want to extract the nitre, you muft proceed with this mixture as with the powder at firft, by which means you will draw out all the faltpetre; but this procefs muft be boiled longer than the firft.

Sulphur, or Brimstone.

Sulphur is by nature the food of fire, and one of the principal ingredients in gunpowder, and almoft in all compofitions of fireworks ; therefore great care muft be taken of its being good, and brought to the higheft perfection. To know when the fulphur is good, you are to obferve that it is of a high yellow, and if, when held in one's hand. it crackles and bounces, it is a fign that it is frefh and good : but as the method of reducing brimftone to a powder is very troublefome, it is better to buy the flour ready made, which is done in large quantities, and in great perfection : but when a grand collection of fireworks are to be made, the ftrongeft and beft fulphur is the lump brimftone ground in the fame manner as gunpowder, which you will find in the following part.

To prepare Charcoal for Fireworks.

Charcoal is a prefervative by which the faltpetre and the brimftone is made into gun-powder, by preventing the fulphur from fuffocating the ftrong and windy exhalation of the nitre. There are feveral forts of wood made ufe of for this purpofe; fome prefer hazle, others willow and alder; but there being fo little difference, you may ufe either, which is moft convenient to be got. And the method of burning it is, Cut it in pieces about 1 or 2 feet long, then fplit each piece in 4 parts;

fcale

scale off the bark and hard knots, and dry them in the
sun or in an oven, then make in the earth a square hole,
and line it with bricks, in which lay the wood, croffing
one another, and set it on fire; when thoroughly lighted and in a flame, cover the hole with boards, and fling
earth over them close, to prevent the air from getting in,
yet fo as not to fall among the charcoal; and when it
has lain thus 24 hours, take out the coals and lay them
in a dry place for use. It is to be obferved, that charcoal for fireworks muft always be foft and well burnt,
which may be bought ready done.

To make Artificial CAMPHOR.

Camphor, in the Materia medica, " is a body of a
" particular nature, being neither a refin, a volatile
" falt, an oil, a juice, a bitumen, or a gum, but a
" mixed fubitance, dry, white, tranfparent and brittle,
" of a ftrong and penetrating fmell. The Indians dif-
" tinguifh two kinds of it, a finer and a coarfer; the
" finer is the produce of Borneo and Sumatra, is very
" rare, and is hardly ever fent into Europe; the coarfer
" is the Japonefe, which is the common, both in the
" Indies and in Europe.

" The camphor, which we meet with in fhops, is
" alfo of 2 kinds, differing in regard to the degree
" of their purity, and diftinguifhed by the name of
" Rough and Refined. The tree, which produces cam-
" phor, is a fpecies of bay tree, every part of which
" abounds with camphor; but is not collected from
" it in the manner of refins, but by a fort of chemical
" procefs.— The natives of the place where the trees
" grow, cut the wood and roots into fmall pieces,
" and put them into large copper veffels, which they
" cover with earthen heads, filled with ftraw; they
" give a moderate fire under them, and the camphor is
" raifed in form of a white downy matter, and retained
" among the ftraw; when the procefs is over, they
                                      " fhake

" fhake it out of the ftraw, and knead it into cakes.
" Thefe cakes are not very compact, but eafily crum-
" bled to pieces; they are moderately heavy, of a
" greyifh or dufky reddifh white in colour, of a pun-
" gent fmell and acrid tafte, and what we call rough
" camphor.

" Refined camphor muft be chofen of a perfectly
" clean white colour, very bright and pellucid, of the
" fame fmell and tafte with the rough, but more acrid
" and pungent.—It is fo volatile that merchants ufually
" inclofe it in lin-feed, that the vifcofity of that grain
" may keep its particles together."

There is alfo an artificial camphor for fireworks,
which is made from gum fandarach pulverifed 2 pound,
and diftilled vinegar enough to cover it; put them
in a glafs phial, and fet it 20 days in warm horfedung.
Then take it out, and pour it into a large-mouth phial;
and expofe it to the fun a month, and you will have a
concreted camphor in form of the cruft of bread, and
fomething like the natural camphor : which when you
ufe muft be ground to a powder with a little fpirits of
wine in a mortar. Though we have here taught the
method of making artificial camphor, I would not
recommend it to thofe who chufe to make their works
to perfection, the natural camphor being by far the
beft.

To make the OIL of CAMPHOR,

Which is fometimes ufed to moiften compofitions.
It is produced by adding to fome camphor a little oil of
fweet almonds, and working them together in a brafs
mortar, till it turns to a green oil.

N. B. Thofe works that have any camphor in their
compofitions, fhould be kept as much from air as poffible, or the camphor will evaporate.

BEN-

BENJAMIN.

Benjamin is a resin (much used by perfumers, and sometimes in medicine); it is brought from the Indies, where it is found of different sorts; and distinguished by colours, viz. yellow, grey, and brown; but the best is that which is easy to break and full of white spots.

Benjamin is one of the ingredients in odoriferous fire-works, when reduced to a fine flour; which may be done by putting into a deep and narrow earthen pot, 3 or 4 oz. of benjamin grossly pounded; cover the pot with paper, which tie very close round the edge; then set the pot on a slow fire, and once in an hour take off the paper, and you will find some flour sticking to it, which return again in the pot; this you must continue till the flour appears white and fine. There is also an oil of benjamin, which is sometimes drawn from the dregs of the flour; it affords a very good scent, and may be used in wet compositions.

ORIGIN of GUN-POWDER.

Gun-powder being the principal ingredient in fire-works, it is proper to give a short definition of its strange explosive force, and cause of action, which, according to Dr. Shaw, the chemical cause of the explosive force of gun-powder, is, " Each grain of powder consisting
" of a certain proportion of sulphur, nitre, and coal,
" the coal presently takes fire, upon contact of the
" smallest spark: at which time both the sulphur and
" the nitre immediately melt, and by means of the coal
" interposed between them, burst into flame; which
" spreading from grain to grain, propagates the same
" effect almost instantaneously: whence the whole mass
" of powder comes to be fired; and as nitre contains
" both a large proportion of air and water, which are
" now violently rarified by the heat, a kind of fiery
                                                " explosive

" explosive blaft is thus produced, wherein the nitre
" feems, by its aqueous and aërial parts, to act as bel-
" lows to the other inflammable bodies, fulphur and
" coal, to blow them into a flame, and carry off their
" whole fubftance in fmoke and vapour."

After having fpoke of the nature of powder, I fhall
in the next place proceed to its origin, though fomewhat uncertain; but it is imagined to have been invented in the time of Alexander the Great, as Philoftratus
fpeaks of a city near the river Hypafis in the Indies, that
was faid to be impregnable, and its inhabitants relations
of the gods, becaufe they threw thunder and lightning
on their enemies; but this perhaps might be the effect
of gun-powder, which, not being known to other people, might well be faid to be thunder and lightning.

This conjecture has been confirmed by fome travellers, who affert that it was ufed in the Eaft-Indies, particularly in the Philippine Iflands, about 85, which
is 1265 years before it was known in Europe, where
they fay it was not known till 1350, though, it is faid,
there is mention made of gunpowder in the regifters of
the chambers of accounts in France, in 1338; and
Friar Bacon mentions the compofition of powder in ex-
prefs terms, in his treatife De nullitate magiae, publifh-
ed at Oxford in 1216; but we find from moft accounts,
that the Germans have the honour of the invention.

I fhould give a defcription of a machine for trying
gun-powder, but they are fo common, it would be
needlefs; yet would have all who practife this art
know, that, when they make fky rockets with powder,
it muft be of the beft kind; but as to wheels, and
other common works, any will do, only be careful it is
quite dry.

Com-

Compoſitions for GUN-POWDER of different kinds.

Having treated of the nature of powder, and its origin, I ſhall give the proportion of each ingredient, it being proper that every one who uſes powder, ſhould know of what it is compoſed Therefore, I ſhall ſet down the ſeveral compoſitions mentioned in Caſimir Siemienowicz's grand art of artillery, in which there are ſix ſorts, viz.

I.			25 lb.		25 lb.
II.			18 lb.		20 lb.
III.	Saltpetre 100 lb. ſulphur		12 lb.	and coal	15 lb.
IV.			20 lb.		24 lb.
V.			15 lb.		18 lb.
VI.			10 lb.		8 lb.

Belidor, in his Hydraulics, ſpeaks of a compoſion for gun-powder, which is, to 30 lb. of ſaltpetre, add 5 lb. of ſulphur, with as much coal: but the proportions of the ſeveral ingredients are to be found beſt by experience.   Though there has been ſo much practice in making powder, there has not yet been aſcertained a ſtanding proportion of the nitre, ſulphur, and coal; but it is hoped that in time this great and noble invention will be much improved, and that the different and beſt quantity of every ingredient will be aſcertained.   At the powder mills they generally allow for waſting, in making up, 1 ½ lb. in 100. Their mixture for 100 of good powder is thus: To 76 ½ lb. of ſaltpetre, well refined and dry'd, 12 ½ lb. of coal, and as much ſulphur, which makes 101 ½ lb. which when worked up will nearly weigh 100. As gun-powder is capable of being improved, I ſhall not omit any particular that may be of ſervice to ſuch as are willing to make experiments; viz. refined ſaltpetre 5 lb. ſulphur 1 lb. 4 oz. and charcoal 7 ½ oz.

Though

Though you may have a good proportion of ingredients, the powder will not always be the fame: much depends on their being well incorporated, corned and dry'd, the method of which will be taught in the next article.

To reftore damaged Gun-powder to its proper ftrength.

It is certain, that, if powder is kept long in a damp place, it will become weak, and great part formed into hard lumps, a fure fign of its being damaged. When powder is thus found, you will fee at the bottom of the barrel fome faltpetre, which, by being wet, will feparate from the fulphur and coal, and fall to the bottom of the veffel, and fettle in the form of a white downey matter; but the only method to prevent this, is to move the barrels as oft as convenient, and place them on their oppofite fides or ends: but though the greateft care be taken, length of time will greatly leffen its primitive ftrength.

Therefore when any of thefe accidents happens, you may recover it by applying to thefe directions; for example, if you imagine that it has not received much damage, proceed thus. Spread it on canvas, or dry boards, and expofe it to the fun, then add to it an equal quantity of good powder, and mix them well, and, when thoroughly dry, barrel, and put it in a dry and proper place. But if gun-powder is quite bad, the method to reftore it is; firft, you muft know what it weighed when good; then, by weighing it again, you find how much it has loft by the feparation and evaporation of the faltpetre; then add to it as much refined faltpetre, as it has wafted, but as a large quantity of this would be difficult to mix, it will be beft to put a proportion of nitre to every 20lb. of powder; when done, put one of thefe proportions into your mealing table, and grind it, till you have brought it to an impalpable powder, then fearce it with a fine fieve; but if

any

any remain in the fieve that will not pafs, return it to
the table, and grind it again, till you have made it all
fine enough to go through ; being thus well ground and
fifted, it muft be made into grains thus : firft you muft
have fome (copper wire fieves) made to what fize you
intend the grains fhould be ; thefe are called corning
fieves or grainers, which fill with the powder compofition, then fhake them about, and the powder will
pafs through the fieve, formed into grains. Having
thus corned it, fet it to dry in the fun ; and when quite
dry, fearce it with a fine hair fieve, to feparate the duft
from the grains. This duft may be worked with another mixture ; fo that none will be wafted : but fometimes it may happen, that the weight when good cannot be known ; in which cafe add to each lb. 1 oz. or
1 $\frac{1}{2}$ oz. of faltpetre, according as the powder is decayed,
and then grind, fift, and granulate it as before.

N. B. If you have a large quantity of powder, that
is very bad, and quite fpoiled ; the only way is to extract the faltpetre from it, according to the ufual manner : for powder thus circumftanced, will be very difficult to recover.

SILENT POWDER, commonly called WHITE POWDER.

It would be rather abfurd to imagine, that it is poffible for gun-powder to have any effect without fome
report, when it is well known, that the found does not
proceed from the powder only, but from the air being
rarified by the expanfion of it.

It is evident, that any compofition acting with the
fame explofive force, will produce the fame effect, in
every refpect. Yet for fuch I never had any proof, nor
ever knew any experiment made of it, but have fo little
faith in it, that I fhould not have given it a place in
this work, had it not been treated of by fome authors
of note ; and at the fame time giving every one, who

is

is fond of this art, all opportunities of making experiments, and of knowing every thing relating to it.

To make SILENT POWDER.

For the firſt ſort, mix 2 lb. of borax, with 4 lb. of gun-powder,

2d. Add ½ lb. of lapis-calaminaris, and ½ lb. of borax, to 2 lb. of powder.

3d. To 6 lb. of gun-powder ½ lb. of calcined moles, with as much borax of Venice.

4th. To 6 ½ lb. of ſaltpetre, 8 ½ lb. of ſulphur, and ½ lb. of the ſecond bark of an elder tree, burnt and ground to a powder, with 2 lb. of common ſalt.

There are many other methods of making ſilent powder, according to report, by uſing camphor or touchwood inſtead of charcoal, or by adding to the common powder burnt paper, hay ſeed, &c. When any of theſe ingredients are to be mixed with common powder, grind them together, and make them into grains.

GUN-POWDER of different Colours.

Notwithſtanding the repeated trials and experiments, made by the greateſt artiſts, to add to the ſtrength of gun-powder, all have proved ineffectual, and moſt have agreed that the preſent powder will not admit of a fourth ingredient: therefore it is evident, that any thing being mixed with the preſent compoſition would rather reduce its ſtrength than add to it; conſequently coloured powder muſt be weaker than black: ſo that the making of powder of different colours, is only a fancy that ſerves to pleaſe the curious, without any other effect.

To make GUN-POWDER white.

To 6 lb. of ſalt-petre, add 1 lb. of the pith of an elder tree, well dried and pulveriſed, with a ſufficient quantity

tity of brimstone to make it into powder, which you will find in the composition of gun-powder, or 1 oz. of the salt of tartar, calcined till it comes white, and then boiled in clear water, till the water is all evaporated.

To make POWDER red.

Boil in water some brasil wood or vermillion and 1 lb. of chopped paper; and, when boiled for some time to draw out the colour, dry and meal it with 1 lb. of sulphur, and 8 lb of saltpetre.

Or, to 6 lb. of saltpetre, 1 lb. of sulphur, and ¼ lb. of amber, and blood stone 1 lb.

To make Yellow POWDER.

Take 8 lb. of saltpetre, 1 lb. of sulphur, and 1 lb. of wild saffron, that has been boiled in aqua vitæ, and afterwards made dry and mealed.

To make Green POWDER.

Boil 2 lb. of rotten wood, with some verdegrease in aqua vitæ, then dry and pound it, and mix it with 1 lb. of sulphur, and 10 lb. of saltpetre.

To make Blue POWDER.

Boil some indigo in aqua vitæ, with 1 lb. of the bark of a young linden tree, then dry and reduce it to a powder, and mix it with 1 lb. of brimstone, and 8 lb. of saltpetre.

To make Pulvis Fulminans, or Thunder in a Room.

This composition is simple, yet has a very curious effect; it is made 3 parts of saltpetre, 2 of salt of tartar, and 1 of sulphur, all ground to a fine powder, and well mixt. As the effect of this powder is quite different from

that

that of gun-powder, so is there a different method of firing it, which is thus: Put about 2 tea spoonfulls of it into a fire-shovel, or iron ladle, and set it over a slow fire, and when it is quite hot, it will go off with a violent report. There is something surprising in the nature of this composition; for as the common powder acts every way equal, and makes the greatest noise when confined, this, on the contrary, acts only downwards, and makes the strongest report when not confined.

There is another sort of fulminating powder, called fulminans aurum, on account of there being gold mixed in its composition, which is done by a chemical preparation; but as the preparing of the ingredients requires a tedious and expensive process, I shall omit the method of doing it, and let those who chuse to make chemical experiments refer to authors on that subject, by whom they will find the manner of making it. It is said one grain of fulminans aurum, when made to perfection, and held on the point of a knife, over a candle, will make a report louder than a musket.

SECT. II.———SPUR-FIRE.

THIS fire is the most beautiful and curious of any yet known, and was invented by the Chinese, but now is in greater perfection in England than in China. As it requires great trouble to make it to perfection, it will be necessary that beginners should have full instructions; therefore care should be taken that all the ingredients are of the best, that the lamp-black is not damp and clodded, that the saltpetre and brimstone are thoroughly refined. This composition is generally rammed in 1 or 2 ounce cases, about 5 or 6 inches long, but not drove very hard; and the cases must have their concave stroke struck very smooth, and the choak or vent not quite so large as the usual proportion; this charge, when driven and kept a few months, will be much better than
when

when rammed, but will not fpoil, if kept dry, in many years.

As the beauty of this compofition cannot be feen at fo great a diftance as brilliant fire, it has a better effect in a room than in the open air, and may be fired in a chamber without any danger : it is of fo innocent a nature, that, though with an improper phrafe, it may be called a cold fire ; and fo extraordinary is the fire produced from this compofition, that, if well made, the fparks will not burn a handkerchief, when held in the midft of them ; you may hold them in your hand while burning, with as much fafety as a candle ; and if you put your hand within a foot of the mouth of the cafe, you will feel the fparks like drops of rain. When any of thefe fpur-fires are fired fingly, they are called artificial flower pots ; but fome of them placed round a tranfparent pyramid of paper, and fired in a large room, make a very pretty appearance.

Compofition for the SPUR-FIRE.

Saltpetre 4 lb. 8 oz. fulphur 2 lb. and lamp-black 1 lb. 8 oz.

Or, faltpetre 1 lb. fulphur ½ lb. and lamp-black 4 quarts.

The fpur-fire compofition being very difficult to mix, and the manner of doing it quite different from any other, I fhall here treat of it feparately ; for example, the falt-petre and the brimftone muft be firft fifted together, and then put into a marble mortar, and the lamp-black with them, which you work down by degrees, with a wooden peftle, till all the ingredients appear of one colour, which will be fomething greyifh, but very near black ; then drive a little into a cafe for trial, and fire it in a dark place ; and if the fparks, which are called ftars. or pinks, come out in clufters, and afterwards fpread well without any other fparks, it is a fign of its being good, otherwife not ; for if any droffy fparks appear, and the ftars not full, it is then not mixed enough ; but if the pinks are

very

very fmall, and foon break, it is a fign that you have rubbed it too much.

N. B. This mixture, when rubbed too much, will be too fierce, and hardly fhew any ftars; and, on the contrary, when not mixed enough, will be too weak, and throw out an obfcure fmoke, and lumps of drofs, without any ftars. The reafon of this charge being called the fpur-fire, is becaufe the fparks it yields have a great refemblance to the rowel of a fpur, from whence it takes its name.

Characters to the Ingredients ufed in Fireworks.

Meal ⎫ Powder ⎰	——— ——— ———	M
Corned ⎭	——— ——— ———	Ɔ
Saltpetre	——— ——— ——— ———	θ
Brimftone	——— ——— ——— ———	Z
Crude Sulphur	——— ——— ——— ———	C Z
Charcoal	——— ——— ——— ———	C +
Sea Coal	——— ——— ——— ———	C S
Saw-duft or Beech-rafpings	——— ———	B R
Steel or Iron filings	——— ——— ———	S X
Brafs ⎫ ⎧	——— ——— ———	B X
Glafs ⎬ duft ⎨	——— ——— ———	G X
Tanners ⎭ ⎩ of Bark	——— ———	T X
Caft Iron	——— ——— ———	C I
Antimony Crude	——— ——— ———	C A
Camphor	——— ———	x
Yellow Amber	——— ——— ———	A Y
Lapis Calaminaris	——— ——— ———	L S
Gum	——— ——— ——— ———	⌒
Lamp Black	——— ———	B L
Ifing Glafs	——— ——— ———	G I
Spirit ⎫ of ⎧ Wine	——— ——— ———	W
Spirits ⎭ ⎩ Turpentine	——— ———	S T
Oil of Spike	——— ——— ——— ———	P Q

Their

Their ufe is, that by them the receipts may be con-tracted, fo that they may be contained in a leaf of a pocket book, which is much lefs than any table that has yet been invented. And they are convenient for travellers.

To meal Gun-powder, Brimstone, and Charcoal.

There have been many methods ufed to grind thefe ingredients to a powder for fireworks, fuch as large mor-tars and peftles, made of ebony, and other hard wood; and horizontal mills with brafs barrels; but none have proved fo effectual and fpeedy as the laft invention, that of the mealing table, reprefented in Plate I. Fig. 1. made of elm, with a rim round its edge, 4 or 5 inches high; and at the narrow end, A, is a flider, that runs in a groove and forms part of the rim; fo that when you have taken out of the table, as much powder as you can, with the copper fhovel Fig. 2. fweep all clean out at the flider A. When you are going to meal a quantity of powder, obferve not to put too much in the table at once; but when you have put in a good proportion, take the muller, Fig. 3. and rub it till all the grains are broke; then fearce it, in a lawn fieve that has a receiver and top to it; and that which does not pafs through the fieve, return again to the table and grind it, till you have brought it all fine enough to go through the fieve. Brimftone and charcoal are ground in the fame manner, only the muller muft be made of ebony; for thefe ingredients, being harder than powder, would ftick in the grain of elm, and be difficult to grind; as brimftone is apt to ftick and clod to the table, it will be beft to keep one for that purpofe, by which means you will always have your brimftone clean and well ground.

To

To prepare Cast-Iron for Gerbes, White Fountains, and Chinese Fire.

Caft-iron being of fo hard a nature, as not to be cut by a file, we are obliged to reduce it into grains, though fomewhat difficult to perform; but if we confider what beautiful fparks this fort of iron yields, no pains fhould be fpared to granulate fuch an effential material, to do which, get at an iron foundry fome thin pieces of iron, fuch as generally runs over the moulds at the time of cafting: then have a fquare block made of caft iron, and an iron fquare hammer about 4 lb. weight; then, having covered the floor with cloth, or fomething to catch the beatings, lay the thin pieces of iron on the block, and beat them with the hammer, till reduced into fmall grains, which afterwards fearce with a very fine fieve, to feparate the fine duft, which is fometimes ufed in fmall cafes of Brilliant fire, inftead of fteel duft; and when you have got out all the duft, fift what remains with a fieve a little larger, and fo on with fieves of different fizes, till the iron paffes through about the bignefs of fmall bird fhot: your iron thus beat and fifted, put each fort into wooden boxes or oiled paper, to keep it from rufting. When you ufe it, obferve the difference of its fize, in proportion to the cafes for which the charge is intended; for the coarfe fort is only defigned for very large gerbes, of 6, 6, or 8 lb.

Charges for Sky-Rockets, &c.

Rockets of Four Ounces.

Mealed powder 1 lb. 4 oz. faltpetre 4 oz. and charcoal 2 oz.

C   Rockets

Rockets of Eight Ounces.

I. Mealed powder 1 lb. saltpetre 4 oz. brimstone 3 oz. and charcoal 1 oz. and ½.

II. Meal powder 1 lb. and ½, and charcoal 4 oz. and ¼.

Rockets of One Pound.

Meal powder 2 lb. saltpetre 8 oz. brimstone 4 oz. charcoal 2 oz. and steel filings 1 oz. and ½.

Sky Rockets in general.

I. Saltpetre 4 lb. brimstone 1 lb. and charcoal 1 lb. ¼.

II. Saltpetre 4 lb. brimstone 1 lb. ½. charcoal 1 lb. 12 oz. and meal powder 2 oz.

Large Sky Rockets.

Saltpetre 4 lb. meal powder 1 lb. and brimstone 1 lb.

Compositions to be used in Rockets of a middling size.

I. Saltpetre 8 lb. sulphur 3 lb. meal powder 3 lb.

II. Saltpetre 3 lb. sulphur 2 lb. meal powder 1 lb. charcoal 1 lb.

Compositions for Rocket Stars.

White Stars.

Meal powder 4 oz. saltpetre 12 oz. sulphur vivum 6 oz. oil of spike 2 oz. and camphor 5 oz.

Blue Stars.

Meal powder 8 oz. salpetre 4, sulphur 2, spirits of wine 2, and oil of spike 2.

Coloured

Coloured, or variegated Stars.

Meal powder 8 drams, rochpetre 4 oz. sulphur vivum 2, and camphor 2.

Brilliant Stars.

Saltpetre 3 ½ oz. sulphur 1½, and meal powder ½, worked up with spirits of wine only.

Common Stars.

Saltpetre 1lb. brimstone 4 oz. antimony 4 ½, isinglass ½, camphor ½, and spirits of wine ¼.

Tailed Stars.

Meal powder 3 oz. brimstone 2, saltpetre 1½, and charcoal (coarsely ground) ½.

Drove Stars.

I. Saltpetre 3lb. sulphur 1lb. brass dust 12 oz. antimony 3.

II. Saltpetre 1lb. antimony 4 oz. and sulphur 8.

Fixed Pointed Stars.

Saltpetre 8 ½ oz. sulphur 2, antimony 1 oz. 10 dr.

Stars of a Fine Colour.

Sulphur 1 oz. meal powder 1, saltpetre 1, camphor 4 dr. oil of turpentine 4 dr.

Gold Rain for Sky Rockets.

I. Saltpetre 1lb. meal powder 4 oz. sulphur 4, brass dust 1, saw dust 2 ½, and glass dust 6 dr.

II. Meal powder 12 oz. saltpetre 2, charcoal 4.

C 2   III.

III. Saltpetre 8 oz. brimstone 2, glass dust 1, antimony ½, brass dust ½, and saw dust 12 dr.

Silver Rain.

I. Saltpetre 4 oz. sulphur, meal powder, and antimony, of each 2 oz. sal prunella ½ oz.

II. Saltpetre ½lb. brimstone 2 oz. and charcoal 4.

III. Saltpetre 1lb. brimstone ½lb. antimony 6 oz.

IV. Saltpetre 4 oz. brimstone 1, powder 2, and steel dust ½ oz.

Water Rockets.

I. Meal powder 6lb. saltpetre 4, brimstone 3, charcoal 5.

II. Saltpetre 1lb. brimstone 4½ oz. charcoal 6.

III. Saltpetre 1lb. brimstone 4 oz. charcoal 12 oz.

IV. Saltpetre 4lb. brimstone 1lb. 8 oz. charcoal 1lb. 12 oz.

V. Brimstone 2lb. saltpetre 4lb. and meal powder 4.

VI. Saltpetre 1lb. meal powder 4 oz. brimstone 8 ½, charcoal 2.

VII. Meal powder 1lb. saltpetre 3, brimstone 1. seacoal 1 oz. charcoal 8½, saw dust ½, steel dust ½, and coarse charcoal ½ oz.

VIII. Meal powder 1½lb. saltpetre 3, sulphur 1½, charcoal 12 oz. saw dust 2.

Sinking Charge for Water Rockets.

Meal powder 8 oz. charcoal ¼ oz.

Wheel Cases from 2 oz. to 4lb.

I. Meal powder 2lb. saltpetre 4 oz. iron filings 7.

II. Meal powder 2lb. saltpetre 12 oz. sulphur 4, steel dust 3.

III. Meal powder 4lb. saltpetre 1lb. brimstone 8 oz. charcoal 4 ½.

IV.

IV. Meal powder 8 oz. saltpetre 4, faw duft 1½, feacoal ¼.

V. Meal powder 1lb. 4 oz. brimftone 4 oz. 10 dr. faltpetre 8 oz. glafs duft 2½.

VI. Meal powder 12 oz. charcoal 1, faw duft ½.

VII. Saltpetre 1lb. 9 oz. brimftone 4 oz. charcoal 4½.

VIII. Meal powder 2lb. faltpetre 1, brimftone ½, and feacoal 2 oz.

IX. Saltpetre 2lb. brimftone 1, meal powder 4, and glafs duft 4 oz.

X. Meal powder 1lb. faltpetre 2 oz. and fteel duft 3½.

XI. Meal powder 2lb. and fteel duft 2½ oz. with 2½ of the fine duft of beat iron.

XII. Saltpetre 2lb. 13 oz. brimftone 8 oz. and charcoal 6.

Slow Fire for Wheels.

I. Saltpetre 4 oz. brimftone 2, and meal powder 1½.

II. Saltpetre 4 oz. brimftone 1, and antimony 1 oz. 6 dr.

III. Saltpetre 4½ oz. brimftone 1 oz. and mealed powder 1½.

Dead Fire for Wheels.

I. Saltpetre 1½ oz. brimftone ½, lapis-calaminaris ½, and antimony 2 dr.

Standing or fixed Cafes.

I. Meal powder 4lb. faltpetre 2, brimftone and charcoal ½.

II. Meal powder 2lb. faltpetre 1, and fteel duft 8 oz.

III. Meal powder 1lb. 4 oz. and charcoal 4 oz.

IV. Meal powder 1lb. and fteel duft 4 oz.

V. Meal powder 2½lb. brimftone 4 oz. and fea coal 6.

VI. Meal powder 3 lb. charcoal 5 oz. and faw duft 1½.

Sun

Sun Cafes.

I. Meal powder 8 ½lb. faltpetre 1 lb. 2 oz. fteel duft 2lb. 10½ oz. brimftone 4.

II. Meal powder 3lb. faltpetre 6 oz. and fteel duft 7½.

A Brilliant Fire.

Meal powder 1½lb. faltpetre 1, brimftone 4 oz. fteel duft 1 ½lb.

Gerbes.

Meal powder 6lb. and beat iron 2lb. 1 ½ oz.

Chinefe Fire.

Saltpetre 12 oz. meal powder 2lb. brimftone 1 lb. 2 oz. and beat iron 12 oz.

Charge for Four-ounce Tourbillons.

Meal powder 2lb. 4 oz. and charcoal 4 ½ oz.

Eight-ounce Tourbillons.

Meal powder 2lb. and charcoal 4 ½ oz.

Large Tourbillons.

Meal powder 2lb. faltpetre 1, brimftone 8 oz. and beat iron 8.

N. B. Tourbillons may be made very large, and of different colour'd fires, only you are to obferve, that the larger they are, the weaker muft be the charge; and, on the contrary, the fmaller, the ftronger their charge.

Water Balloons.

I. Saltpetre 4lb. brimftone 2, meal powder 2, antimony 4 oz. faw duft 4, and glafs duft 1 ½.

II.

II. Saltpetre 9 lb. brimstone 3 lb. meal powder 6 lb. rosin 12 oz. and antimony 8 oz.

Water Squibs.

I. Meal powder 1 lb. and charcoal 1 lb.

II. Meal powder 1 lb. and charcoal 9 oz.

Mine Ports or Serpents.

I. Meal powder 1 lb. and charcoal 1 oz.

II. Meal powder 9 oz. charcoal 1 oz.

Port-fires for firing Rockets, &c.

I. Saltpetre 12 oz. brimstone 4 oz. and meal powder 2 oz.

II. Saltpetre 8 oz. brimstone 4 oz. and meal powder 2 oz.

III. Saltpetre 1 lb. 2 oz. meal powder 1½ lb. and brimstone 10 oz. This composition must be moistened with one gill of linseed oil.

IV. Meal powder 6 oz. saltpetre 2 lb. 2 oz. and brimstone 10 oz.

V. Saltpetre 1 lb. 4 oz. meal powder 4 oz. brimstone 5 oz. saw dust 8 oz.

VI. Saltpetre 8 oz. brimstone 2 oz. and meal powder 2 oz.

Port-fires for Illuminations.

Saltpetre 1 lb. brimstone 8 oz. and meal powder 6 oz.

Cones or Spiral Wheels.

Saltpetre 1½ lb. brimstone 6 oz. meal powder 4 oz. and glass dust 14 oz.

Crowns, or Globes.

Saltpetre 6 oz. brimstone 2 lb. antimony 4 oz. and camphor 2 oz.

Air

Air Balloon Fuzes.

I. Saltpetre 1 lb. 10 oz. brimstone 8 oz. and meal powder 1 lb. 6 oz.

II. Saltpetre 1½ lb. brimstone 8 oz. and meal powder 1 lb. 8 oz.

Serpents for Pots des Brins.

Meal powder 1 lb. 8 oz. saltpetre 12 oz. and charcoal 2 oz.

Fire Pumps.

I. Saltpetre 5 lb. brimstone 1 lb. meal powder 1 lb. and glass dust 1 lb.

II. Saltpetre 5 lb. 8 oz. brimstone 2 lb. meal powder 1 lb. 8 oz. and glass dust 1 lb. 8 oz.

A Slow White Flame.

I. Saltpetre 2 lb. sulphur 3 lb. antimony 1 lb.

II. Saltpetre 3½ lb. sulphur 2½ lb. meal powder 1 lb. antimony ½ lb. glass dust 4 oz. brass dust 1 oz.

N. B. These compositions, driven 1¾ inch in a 1 oz. case, will burn 1 minute, which is much longer time than an equal quantity of any composition, yet known, will last.

Amber Lights.

Meal powder 9 oz. amber 3 oz. This charge may be drove in small cases, for illuminations.

Lights of another Kind.

Saltpetre 3 lb. brimstone 1 lb. meal powder 1 lb. antimony 10½ oz. All these must be mixed with the oil of spike.

A Red Fire.

Meal powder 3 lb. charcoal 12 oz. and faw duft 8 oz.

A Common Fire.

Saltpetre 3 lb. charcoal 10 oz. and brimftone 2 oz.

To make an Artificial Earthquake.

Mix the following ingredients to a pafte with water, and then bury it in the ground, and in a few hours the earth will break and open in feveral places. The compofition: Sulphur 4 lb. and fteel duft 4 lb.

Having laid down, under the preceding heads, the different compofitions ufed in fireworks by our modern artifts; I fhall, in the next place, give fome tables of charges that were formerly ufed, according to the feveral accounts given by thofe authors from whom they are collected: but if the reader will confider, he will find the charges in thefe tables to be very uncertain, by comparing their method of determining the fize and weight of rockets, and the proportions of ingredients thereto, with the method taught in this work, which is fo plain, eafy, and certain, that I never yet knew it fail; and doubt not, but that it will be fo allowed by all who chufe to make the trial.

The fubfequent table is taken from Siemienowicz, wherein are fpecified the different charges of fky rockets, from ½ oz. to 100 lb.; the charges being calculated in proportion to the weight of a leaden ball of the fame diameter as the bore of each mould; which bores are divided into inches and lines,* and each line into 12 parts, according to the French method.

* A line is the 12th part of an inch.

TAB. I.

TAB. I.

Charges for Rockets, &c.

Ball's weight.		Mould's diam.			Powder.		Salt-petre.		Brimstone.		Charcoal.	
lb.	oz.	in.	l.	pts.	lb.	oz.	lb.	oz.	lb.	oz.	lb.	oz.
	½	0	6	3								
	1	0	7	8	0	15	0	0	0	0	0	2
	2	0	9	7								
	3	0	11	0	0	12	0	2	0	½	0	1¼
	4	1	0	1								
	5	1	1	0								
	6	1	1	10	1	3	0	12	0	4	0	1¼
	7	1	2	7								
	8	1	3	4								
	9	1	3	11								
	10	1	4	5								
	11	1	5	0								
	12	1	5	5								
	13	1	6	0								
	14	1	6	5								
	16	1	7	3	18	0	8	0	2	0	4	0
2	0	2	0	3	0	0	60	0	2	0	15	0
3	0	2	3	7								
4	0	2	6	9	0	0	64	0	8	0	16	0
5	0	2	8	8								
6	0	2	10	9	0	0	35	0	5	0	10	0
8	0	3	2	6								
10	0	3	5	4	0	0	62	0	9	0	20	0
12	0	3	7	10	0	0	32	0	8	0	16	0
15	0	3	11	4								
17	0	4	1	5	0	0	64	0	12	0	16	0
20	0	4	4	2								
27	0	4	9	9								
30	0	4	11	6	0	0	30	0	7	0	18	0
40	0	5	5	1								
60	0	6	3	3								
100	0	7	5	3	0	0	30	0	10	0	20	0

TAB. II.

Rocket, &c. Charges.

From a late French author*, who regulated his charges according to the interior diameter of the mould, divided into lines.

Interior diameter of the mould.	Rocket's Weight.			Saltpetre.	Brimstone.	Charcoal.
Lines.	lb.	oz.	dr.	ounces.	ounces.	ounces.
6	0	0	4 }			
7	0	0	6 }	44	4	16
8	0	1	1 }			
9	0	1	5 }			
10	0	2	2 }	40	4	16
11	0	3	0 }			
12	0	3	7 }			
13	0	4	6 }	38	4	16
14	0	6	1 }			
15	0	7	4 }			
16	0	9	1 }	36	4	16
17	0	11	0 }			
18	0	13	1 }			
19	0	15	4 }	34	4	16
19½	1	0	0 }			
21	1	7	1 }			
24	1	15	1 }	32	5	16
30	4	0	0 }			
36	6	9	0 }	30	6	18
72	55	8	0 }			

* Traité des feux d'artifice, par M. F***.

TAB.

TAB. III.

SKY-ROCKETS.

The charges adapted to the weight of composition in each, after Hanzelet's method.

Composition Wt.		Powder		Saltpetre		Brimstone		Charcoal	
lb.	oz.	lb.	oz.	lb.	oz.	lb.	oz.	lb.	oz.
0	7½	0	4					0	1
or		1	0	0	1½			0	1½
0	2	1	0	0	1			0	½
or		1	0						
0	4	1	0	0	4			0	4
or		0	8	0	10	0	1	0	3
		0	10	0	3½	0	1	0	3½
1	0	0	1			0	1	0	2
or				1	4	0	2	0	3½
3	0			1	14	7	7½	0	11
6	0			31	0	4	8	10	0
7	0								
8	0			8	0	1	8	2	12
10	0								

TAB. IV.

From Henrion, whose method is as in the preceding.

Composition Wt.	Powder		Saltpetre		Brimstone		Charcoal	
lb. oz.	lb.	oz.	lb.	oz.	lb.	oz.	lb.	oz.
1	1	0					0	2
2								
or,	1	0	1	0			0	1
3		4½	0	½			0	1
4	4	0	1	0	0	½	0	4
8								
	1	8	0	4			0	2
or,	1	0	0	4			0	1
	3	½	0	10			0	3½
8					0	2 steel duft		
	2	5	0	0	0	2	0	6
10								
12	17	0	0	4	0	3½	0	7
14					0	3		
	2	8	0	9	steel duft 0	3	0	3
15					0	3		
1 0	1	0	0	0	0	½	0	3
2 0	0	2	0	12	0	1	0	3
3 0					1	4 steel duft		
	0	0	8	0			2	2
10 0					0	2		

TAB.

TAB. V.

Charges for Sky-Rockets,

From M. de Saint Remy, improved by M. F***.

Composition for a Rocket of

2 lb.	1 lb.	½ lb.	4 oz.	1½ oz.

CORRECTED

By M. F***, 1lb.	11 oz.	7½ oz.	6 oz. 5 dr.	1 oz. 5 dr.
lb. oz.	lb. oz.	lb. oz.	oz.	oz.
Pow. 2 0	1 0	1 4	5	8 or 9⅖
Saltp. 1 0	12	12	$\frac{5}{1}$	$\frac{5}{s}$
Brimst. 5	2	1	¼	
Charc. 4		3	½	¼ or ½
Steel-d. 2		2		

Mould Height, in Inches.

9½ in.	8¼	7½	7	4½

Diameter, in Inches and Lines.

2 in. 7 l.	1 5	1 3	1 2	9 lines

French Names for Sky Rockets.

Double Marquise.	Marquise.	Grosse department	Departement.	Fusée de Caisse

Remarks

Remarks on the foregoing Tables.

In the first, we find that the compositions for all rockets under 1lb. are made chiefly of gunpowder and charcoal, which method has been long proved erroneous in many respects: first, that rockets made with such charges will not keep long without spoiling; secondly, that they are very uncertain in performing their proper effect; thirdly, they will carry but a short tail, with a black and smoaky fire.

We also find those charges for rockets above 1 lb., that are composed of saltpetre, brimstone, and charcoal, to be too strong; by which we should imagine that, at the time when they were used, the piercers did not bear the same proportion to the rockets, as those used by our present artists; as it is on the size of the cavity in the composition, that the effect of the rocket and proportion of the charge depends: which I shall endeavour to shew hereafter.

Table II. is given, by the author, as an improvement on the first; wherein he takes notice of the charges being too many in number; he has therefore reduced them to 7, which, according to his opinion, are sufficient for rockets of any size: he also observes, that the ingredients are expressed in unequal quantities; which he has likewise laid down in a more regular order. By the same author's account, rockets were made in France, not many years since, with the compositions mentioned in his table. I shall not here pretend to say, that rockets were not made with the charges given in the said table; yet can affirm, by experience, that several of them will not agree with our present moulds.

As to the method prescribed in tables III. and IV. it is difficult to determine whether we shall praise or condemn them, as they were wrote when the art of making fireworks was in its infancy; as may be seen by their strange method of determining the proportion of ingredients,

dients, and weight of rockets, by the quantity of composition contained in each case; which must have required a very nice calculation; for at that time they had not fixed upon an exact length for rockets, but made them from 6 to 9 diameters long: all which differ so much from our modern practice, that I never thought it worth the trouble of making a trial; but am of opinion, that very few of the charges will answer.

In the fifth Table, the compositions are in proportion to the weight of the rocket, with its head and stick, all complete; which head and stick are equal to the weight of the rocket, according to the improvement made by M. F***, as in the second column from the top: he has also added the diameters to the moulds, in proportion to their height, allowing each 6 diameters, which supposing to be right, the rockets will be nearly reduced to ¼ their weight given in the first column. On the charges in this table I have made no experiment, therefore cannot recommend them as proof.

Having given a variety of charges for sky-rockets, in the preceding tables, which are collected from the principal authors on this subject, together with remarks, I shall, in the next place, according to my promise of not omitting any thing that may be of service to the reader, add some compositions for rocket-stars of several colours, as inserted by former authors.

Compositions for Stars of different Colours.

I. Meal powder 4 oz. saltpetre 2 oz. brimstone 2 oz. steel dust 1 ½ oz. and camphor, white amber, antimony, and mercury-sublimate, of each ¼ oz.

II. Rochepetre 10 oz. brimstone, charcoal, antimony, meal powder, and camphor, of each ½ oz. moistened with oil of turpentine. These compositions are made into stars, by being worked to a paste with aqua vitæ, in which has been dissolved some gum-tragacanth; and after you have rolled them in powder, make a hole through the middle of each, and string them on quick-match, leaving about 2 inches between each.

III

III. Saltpetre 8 oz. brimstone 2 oz. yellow amber 1 oz. antimony 1 oz. and powder 3 oz.

IV. Brimstone 2 ½ oz. saltpetre 6 oz. olibanum or frankincense in drops 4 oz.; mastick, and mercury-sublimate, of each 4 oz. meal powder 5 oz. white amber, yellow amber, and camphor, of each 1 oz. antimony and orpiment ½ oz. each.

V. Saltpetre 1 lb. brimstone ½ lb. and meal powder 8 oz. moistened with potrolio-oil.

VI. Powder ¼ lb. brimstone and saltpetre, of each 4 oz.

VII. Saltpetre 4 oz. brimstone 2 oz. and meal powder 1 oz.

Stars that carry Tails of Sparks.

I. Brimstone 6 oz. antimony crude 2 oz. saltpetre 4 oz. and rosin 4 oz.

II. Saltpetre, rosin, and charcoal, of each 2 oz. brimstone 1 oz. and pitch 1 oz.

These compositions are sometimes melted in an earthen pan, and mixed with chopped cotton-match, before they are rolled into stars, but will do as well if wetted, and worked up in the usual manner.

Stars that yield some Sparks.

I. Camphor 2 oz. saltpetre 1 oz. meal powder 1 oz.

II. Saltpetre 1 oz. ditto melted ½ oz. and camphor 2 oz. When you would make stars of either of these compositions, you must wet them with gum water, or spirit of wine, in which has been dissolved some gum-arabick, or gum-tragacanth, that the whole may have the consistence of a pretty thick liquid; having thus done, take 1 oz. of lint, and stir it about in the composition till it becomes dry enough to roll into stars.

Stars of a yellowish Colour.

Take 4 oz. of gum-tragacanth or gum-arabick, pounded and sifted through a fine sieve, camphor dissolved

D

in

in brandy 2 oz. faltpetre 1 lb. fulphur ½ lb. coarfe powder of glafs 4 oz. white amber 1 ¼ oz. orpiment 2 oz.
Being well incorporated, make them into ftars after the
common method.

Stars of another Kind.

Take 1 lb. of camphor, and melt it in a pint of fpirit
of wine over a flow fire ; then add to it 1 lb. of gum-
arabick that has been diffolved; with this liquor mix 1lb.
of faltpetre, 6 oz. of fulphur, and 5 oz. of meal powder ; and after you have ftirred them well together, roll
them into ftars proportionable to the rockets for which
you intend them.

Colours produced by the different Com-
pofitions.

As variety of fires adds greatly to a collection of works,
it is neceffary that every artift fhould know the different
effect of each ingredient; for which reafon, I fhall
here explain the colours they produce of themfelves ;
and likewife how to make them retain the fame when
mixed with other bodies: as for example, fulphur gives
a blue, camphor a white or pale colour, faltpetre a
clear white, yellow amber a colour inclining to yellow,
fal-armoniac a green, antimony a reddifh, rofin a copper colour, and greek-pitch a kind of bronze or between red and yellow. All thefe ingredients are fuch
as fhew themfelves in a flame, viz.

White Flame.

Saltpetre, fulphur, meal powder, and camphor; the
faltpetre muft be the chief part.

Blue Flame.

Meal powder, faltpetre, and fulphur vivum ; fulphur
muft be the chief: or, meal powder, faltpetre, brimstone,

ftone, fpirit of wine, and oil of fpike; but let the powder be the principal part.

Flame inclining to Red.

Saltpetre, fulphur, antimony, and greek-pitch; faltpetre the chief.

By the above method may be made various colours of
fire, as the practitioner pleafes; for, by making a few
trials, he may caufe any ingredient to be predominan
in colour.

Ingredients that fhew in Sparks when rammed in choaked Cafes.

The fet colours of fire produced by fparks are divided
into 4 forts, viz. the black, white, grey, and red: the
black charges are compofed of 2 ingredients, which are
meal powder and charcoal; the white of 3, viz.
faltpetre, fulphur, and charcoal; the grey of 4, viz.
meal powder, faltpetre, brimftone, and charcoal; and
the red of 3, viz. meal powder, charcoal, and faw
duft.

There are, befides thefe 4 regular or fet charges,
2 others, which are diftinguifhed by the names of compound and brilliant charges; the compound being made
of many ingredients, fuch as meal powcer, faltpetre,
brimftone, charcoal, faw duft, fea-coal, antimony, glafs
duft, brafs duft, fteel filings, caft iron, tanner's duft,
&c. or any thing that will yield fparks; all which muft
be managed with difcretion. The brilliant fires are compofed of meal powder, faltpetre, brimftone, and fteel
duft; or with meal powder and fteel filings only.

Cotton Quick-match

Is generally made of fuch cotton as is put in can-
dles, of feveral fizes, from 1 to 6 threads thick, according to the pipes it is defigned for, which pipe muft

be

be large enough for the match, when made, to be pushed in easily without breaking it. Having doubled the cotton into as many threads as you think proper, coil it very lightly into a flat-bottomed copper or earthen pan; then put in the saltpetre and the liquor, and boil them about 10 minutes; after which coil it again into another pan, as in Fig. 4. and pour on it what liquor remains; then put in some meal powder, and prefs it down with your hands, till it is quite wet; afterwards place the pan before the wooden frame, Fig. 5. which muft be fufpended by a point in the centre of each end; and place yourfelf before the pan, tying the upper end of the cotton to the end of 1 of the fides of the frame.

When every thing is ready, you muft have one to turn the frame round, while you let the cotton pafs through your hands, holding it very lightly, and at the fame time keeping your hands full of the wet powder; but if the powder fhould be too wet to ftick to the cotton, put more in the pan, fo as to keep a continual fupply till the match is all wound up; you may wind it as clofe on the frame as you pleafe, fo that it does not ftick together; when the frame is full, take it off the points, and fift dry meal powder on both fides the match, till it appears quite dry: in winter the match will be a fortnight before it is fit for ufe; when it is thoroughly dry, cut it along the outfide of one of the fides of the frame, and tie it up in fkains for ufe.

N. B. The match muft be wound tight on the frames.

Ingredients for the Match.

Cotton 1 lb. 12 oz. faltpetre 1 lb. fpirit of wine 2 quarts, water 3 quarts, ifinglafs 3 gills, and meal powder 10 lb. To diffolve 4 oz. of ifinglafs, take 3 pints of water.

SECT.

Sect. III.—Sky-rocket Moulds.

AS the performance of rockets depends much on their moulds, it is requisite to give a definition of them and their proportions: They are made and proportioned by the diameter of their orifice, which are divided into = parts: as Fig 6. reprefents a mould made by its diameter AB, its height from C to D is 6 diameters and 2 thirds; from D to E is the height of the foot, which is 1 diameter and 2 thirds; F the choak, or cylinder, whofe height is 1 diameter and 1-3d; it muft be made out of the fame piece as the foot, and fit tight in the mould; G an iron pin that goes through the mould and cylinder, to keep the foot faft; H the nipple, which is ½ a diameter high, and 2-3ds thick, and of the fame piece of metal as the piercer I, whofe height is 3 ½ diameters, and at the bottom is 1 3d of the diameter thick, and from thence tapering to 1-6th of the diameter: the beft way to fix the piercer in the cylinder, is to make that part below the nipple long enough to go quite through the foot, and rivet it at bottom. Fig. 7. is a former or roller for the cafes, whofe length, from the handle, is 7 ½ diameters, and its diameter 2-3ds of the bore AB; 8. the end of the former, which is of the fame thicknefs, and 1 diameter and 2-3ds long; the fmall part, which fits into the hole in the end of the roller when the cafe is pinching, is 1 6th and ½ of the mould's diameter thick. Fig. 9. the firft drift, which muft be 6 diameters from the handle, and this as well as all other rammers muft be a little thinner than the former, to prevent the facking of the paper, when you are driving in the charge: in the end of this rammer is a hole to fit over the piercer; the line K marked on this is 2 diameters and 1-3d from the handle; fo that, when you are filling the rocket, this line appears at top of the cafe; you muft then take the 2d rammer, 10. which

from

from the handle is 4 diameters; and the hole for the piercer is 1¼ diameter long. Fig 11. is the short and solid drift which you use when you have filled the case as high as the top of the piercer.

Rammers must have a collar of brass at the bottom, to keep the wood from spreading or splitting; and that the same proportion be given to all moulds, from 1 oz. to 6 lb. I mentioned nothing concerning the handles of the rammers; however, if their diameter be equal to the bore of the mould, and 2 diameters long, it will be a very good proportion; but the shorter you can use them, the better; for the longer the drift, the less will be the pressure on the composition, by the blow given with the mallet.

Dimensions for Rocket Moulds, in which the Rockets are rammed solid.

Weight of rockets.		Length of the moulds without their feet.	Interior diameter of the moulds	Height of the nipples.
lb.	oz.	Inches	Inches.	Inches
6	0	34,7	3,5	1,5
4	0	38,6	2,9	1,4
2	0	13,35	2,1	1,0
1	0	12,25	1,7	0,85
0	8	10,125	1,333 &c.	0,6
0	4	7,75	1,125	0,5
0	2	6,2	0,9	0,45
0	1	4,9	0,7	0,35
0	½	3,9	0,55	0,25
6 drams		3,5	0,5	0,225
4 drams		2,2	0,3	0,2

The

The diameter of the nipple muft always be equal to that of the former.

I have omitted the thicknefs of the moulds, it being very immaterial, provided they are fubftantial and ftrong.

I would not advife thofe who make rockets for private amufement, to ram them folid, for it requires a very fkillful hand, and an expenfive apparatus for boring them, which will be fhewn hereafter. Driving of rockets folid is the moft expeditious method, but not fo certain as ramming them over a piercer, which I have found by experience.

Moulds for Wheel Cafes or Serpents.

Fig. 12. reprefents a mould, in which the cafes are drove folid; L the nipple*, with a point† at top, which, when the cafe is filling, ferves to ftop the neck, and prevent the compofition from falling out, which without this point it would do; and, in confequence, the air would get into the vacancy in the charge, and at the time of firing caufe the cafe to burft. Thefe fort of moulds are made of any length or diameter, according as the cafes are required; but the diameter of the rollers muft be equal to half the bore, and the rammers made quite folid.

To roll Rocket and other Cafes.

Sky-rocket cafes are to be made 6¼ of their exterior diameter long, and all other cafes that are to be filled in moulds muft be as long as the moulds, within half its interior diameter.

Rocket cafes, from the fmalleft to 4 or 6 pound, are generally made of the ftrongeft fort of cartridge paper,

* The nipple and cylinder to bear the fame proportion as thofe for rockets.

† A round bit of br. fs, equal in length to the nick of the cafe, and flat at the top.

and

and rolled dry; but the large fort are made of pasted
paste-board. As it is very difficult to roll the ends of
the cases quite even, the best way will be to keep a pattern of the paper for the different forts of cases, which
pattern should be somewhat longer than the cafe it is
designed for, and on it marked the number of sheets
required, which will prevent any paper being cut to
waste: having cut your papers of a proper size, and
the last sheet for each cafe with a slope at one end, so
that when the cases are rolled it may form a spiral line
round the outside, and that this slope may always be the
fame, let the pattern be so cut for a guide: before you
begin to roll, fold down one end of the first sheet, so far
that the fold will go 2 or 3 times round the former;
then, on the double edge, lay the former with its handle
off the table, and when you have rolled on the paper,
within 2 or 3 turns, lay, on that part which is loose, the
next sheet, and roll it all on.

Having thus done, you must have a smooth board,
about 20 inches long, and equal in breadth to the
length of the cafe; in the middle of this board must
be a handle placed length-ways; under this board lay
your cafe, and let one end of the board lie on the table;
then press hard on it, and push it forwards, which will
roll the paper very tight; do this 3 or 4 times before
you roll on any more paper: this must be repeated every
other sheet of paper, till the cafe is thick enough; but
if the rolling board be drawn backwards, it will loosen
the paper: you are to observe, when you roll on the last
sheet, that the point of the slope be placed at the small end
of the roller. Having rolled your cafe to fit the mould,
push in the small end of the former F, about 1 diameter
from the end of the cafe, and put in the end piece within
a little distance of the former; then give the pinching
cord one turn round the cafe, between the former and
the end piece; at first pull easy, and keep moving the
cafe, which will make the neck smooth, and without
large wrinkles; when the cases are hard to choak, let
each sheet of paper (except the first and last, in that
part

part where the neck is formed) be a little moiftened with water: immediately after you have ftruck the concave ftroke, bind the neck of the cafe round with fmall twine, which muft not be tied in a knot, but faftened with 2 or 3 hitches.

Having thus pinched and tied the cafe fo as not to give way, put it into the mould without its foot, and with a mallet drive the former hard on the end piece, which will force the neck clofe and fmooth; this done, cut the cafe to its proper length, allowing from the neck to the edge of the mouth half a diameter, which is = to the height of the nipple; then take out the former, and drive the cafe over the piercer with the long rammer, and the vent will be of a proper fize. Wheel cafes muft be drove on a nipple with a point, to clofe the neck, and make the vent of the fize required; which, in moft cafes, is generally ¼ of their interior diameter: as it is very oft difficult, when the cafes are rolled, to draw the roller out, you may make a hole through the handle, and put in it a fmall iron pin, by which you may eafily turn the former round, and pull it out. Fig. 17. fhews the method of pinching cafes; P a treddle, which, when preffed hard with the foot, will draw the cord tight, and force the neck as clofe as you pleafe; Q a fmall wheel or pully, with a groove round it for the cord to run in.

Cafes are commonly rolled wet, for wheels and fixed pieces; and when they are required to contain a great length of charge, the method of making thofe cafes is thus: Your paper muft be cut as ufual, only the laft fheet muft not be cut with a flope; having your paper ready, pafte each fheet on one fide; then fold down the firft fheet as before directed, but be careful that the pafte does not touch the upper part of the fold, for if the roller be wetted, it will tear the paper in drawing it out: in pafting the laft fheet, obferve not to wet the laft turn or 2 in that part where it is to be pinched; for if that part be damp, the pinching cord will ftick to it, and tear the paper; therefore, when you choak thofe

cafes,

cafes, roll a bit of dry paper once round the cafe, before you put on the pinching cord; but this bit of paper muft be taken off after the cafe is choaked. The rolling board, and all other methods, according to the former directions for the rolling and pinching of cafes, muft be ufed to thefe as well as all other cafes.

T. make Tourbillon Cafes.

Thofe fort of cafes are generally made about 8 diameters long, but if very large, 7 will be fufficient: tourbillons will anfwer very well from 4 oz. to 2 lb. but when larger there is no certainty. The cafes are beft rolled wet with pafte, and the laft fheet muft have a ftrait edge, fo that the cafe may be all of a thicknefs: when you have rolled your cafes, after the manner of wheel cafes, pinch them at one end quite clofe; then, with the rammer, drive the ends down flat, and afterwards ram in about 1-3d of a diameter of dried clay. The diameter of the former for thefe cafes muft be the fame as for fky rockets.

N. B. Tourbillons are to be rammed in moulds without a nipple, or in a mould without its foot.

Ballóon Cafes, or Paper Shells.

Firft you muft have an oval former turned of fmooth wood; then pafte a quantity of brown or cartridge paper, and let it lie till the pafte has quite foaked through; this done, rub the former with foap or greafe, to prevent the paper from fticking to it; then lay the paper on in fmall flips, till you have made it 1-3d of the thicknefs of the fhell intended; having thus done, fet it to dry, and when dry, cut it round the middle, and the 2 halves will eafily come off; but obferve, when you cut, to leave about 1 inch not cut, which will make the halves join much better than if quite feparated; when you have fome ready to join, place the halves even together, and pafte a flip of paper round the opening to hold them together,

together, and let that dry; then lay on paper all over
as before, every where equal, excepting that end
which goes downwards in the mortar, which may be
a little thicker than the reft; for that part which re-
ceives the blow from the powder in the chamber of the
mortar confequently requires the greateft ftrength: when
the fhell is thoroughly dry, burn a round vent at top,
with fquare iron, large enough for the fuze: this method
will do for ballóóns from 4 inches 2-5ths, to 8 inches
diameter; but if they are larger, or required to be thrown
a great height, let the firft fhell be turned of elm, inftead
of being made of paper.

For a ballóón of 4 inches 2-5ths, let the former be
3 inches 1-8th diameter, and 5¼ inches long. For a
ballóón of 5½ inches the diameter of the former muft
be 4 inches, and 8 inches long. For a ballóón of 8 inches,
let the diameter of the former be 5 inches and 15-16ths,
and 11 inches 7-8ths long. For a 10-inch ballóón,
let the former be 7 inches 3-16ths diameter, and 14¼
inches long. The thicknefs of a fhell for a ballóón of
4 inches 2-5ths, muft be ½ inch. For a ballóón of
5½ inches let the thicknefs of the paper be 5-8ths of an
inch. For an 8-inch balloon, 7-8ths of an inch. And
for a 10 inch ballóón, let the fhell be 1 inch 1-8th
thick.

Shells that are defigned for ftars only, may be made
quite round, and the thinner they are at the opening, the
better; for if they are too ftrong, the ftars are apt to
break at the burfting of the fhell: when you are making
the fhell, make ufe of a pair of calibres, or a round
gauge, fo that you may not lay the paper thicker in one
place than another; and alfo to know when the fhell
is of a proper thicknefs. Ballóóns muft always be made
to go eafy into the mortars.

Mixing Compofitions.

The performance of the principal part of fireworks
depends much on the compofitions being well mixed;
therefore

therefore great care must be taken in this part of the work, particularly for the compositions for sky rockets. When you have 4 or 5 pounds of ingredients to mix, which is a sufficient quantity at a time (for a larger proportion will not do so well) first put the different ingredients together; then work them about with your hands, till you think they are pretty well incorporated: after which put them into a lawn sieve with a receiver and top to it; and if, after it is sifted, any remains that will not pass through the sieve, grind it again till fine enough; and if it be twice sifted, it will not be amiss: but the compositions for wheels and common works are not so material, nor need not be so fine. But in all fixed works, from which the fire is to play regular, the ingredients must be very fine, and great care taken in mixing them well together; and observe that, in all compositions wherein are steel or iron filings, the hands must not touch; nor will any works, which have iron or steel in their charge, keep long in damp weather, without being properly prepared, according to the following directions.

To preserve Steel or Iron Filings.

It sometimes may happen, that fireworks may be required to be kept a long time, or sent abroad; neither of which could be done with brilliant fires, if made with filings unprepared; for this reason, that the saltpetre being of a damp nature, it causes the iron to rust, the consequence of which is, that when the works are fired, there will appear but very few brilliant sparks, but instead of them a number of red and drossy sparks; and besides, the charge will be so much weakened, that if this was to happen to wheels, the fire will hardly be strong enough to force them round: but to prevent such accidents, prepare your filings thus. Melt in a glazed earthen pan some brimstone over a slow fire, and when melted throw in some filings; which keep stirring about till they are covered with brimstone: this you must do

while

while it is on the fire; then take it off, and stir it very quick till cold, when you must roll it on a board with a wooden roller, till you have broke it as fine as corn powder; after which sift from it as much of the brimstone as you can. There is another method of preparing filings, so as to keep 2 or 3 months in winter; this may be done by rubbing them between the strongest sort of brown paper which before has been moistened with linseed oil.

N. B. If the brimstone should take fire, you may put it out, by covering the pan close at top: it is not of much signification what quantity of brimstone you use, so that there is enough to give each grain of iron a coat; but as much as will cover the bottom of a pan of about 1 foot diameter, will do for 5 or 6 pound of filings, or cast iron for gerbes.

To drive or ram Sky Rockets, &c.

Rockets drove over a piercer must not have so much composition put in them at a time, as when drove solid, for the piercer, taking up great part of the bore of the case, would cause the rammer to rise too high; so that the pressure of it would not be so great on the composition, nor would it be drove every where equal: to prevent which, observe the following rule; that for those rockets, that are rammed over a piercer, let the ladle* hold as much composition as, when drove, will raise the drift ¼ the interior diameter of the case, and for those drove solid to contain as much as will raise it ¼ the exterior diameter of the case: ladles are generally made to go easy in the case, and the length of the scoop about 1½ of its own diameter.

The charge of rockets must always be drove 1 diameter above the piercer, and on it must be rammed 1-3d. of a diameter of clay, through the middle of which bore a small hole to the composition, that, when the charge is burnt to the top, it may communicate its fire, through

* A copper scoop with a wooden handle.

the

the hole, to the stars in the head : great care must be taken to strike with the mallet, and with an equal force, the same number of strokes to each ladle-full of charge ; otherwise the rockets will not rise with an uniform motion, nor will the composition burn equal and regular ; for which reason they cannot carry a proper tail, for it will break before the rocket has got half way up ; instead of reaching from the ground to the top, where the rocket breaks and disperses the stars, rains, or whatever is contained in the head. When you are ramming, keep the drift constantly turning or moving ; and when you use the hollow rammers, knock out of them the composition now and then, or the piercer will split them : to a rocket of 4 oz. give to each ladle-full of charge 16 strokes: to a rocket of 1 lb. 8 : to a 2-pounder, 36 : to a 4-pounder, 42 : and to a 6-pounder, 56 : but rockets of a larger sort cannot be drove well by hand, but must be rammed with a machine made in the same manner as those for driving piles, which are so very common to be seen, that I shall omit a description.

The method of ramming of wheel cases, or any other sort, in which the charge is drove solid, is much the same as sky rockets ; for the same proportion may be observed in the ladle, and the same number of strokes given, according to their diameters, all cases being distinguished by their diameters: in this manner, a case whose bore is equal to a rocket of 4 oz. is called a 4-oz. case, and that which is equal to an 8-oz. rocket an 8-oz. case, and so on, according to the different rockets.

Having taught the method of ramming cases in moulds ; we shall here say something concerning those filled without moulds ; which method, for strong pasted cases, will do extremely well, and save the expence of making so many moulds. The reader must here observe, when he fills any sort of cases, to place the mould on a perpendicular block of wood, and not on any place that is hollow ; for we have found by experience, that when cases were rammed on driving benches, which were

formerly

formerly ufed, the works frequently mifcarried, on account of the hollow refiftance of the benches, which oft jarred and loofened the charge in the cafes; but this accident has never happened fince the driving blocks* have been ufed.

When cafes are to be filled without moulds, proceed thus; have fome nipples made of brafs or iron, of feveral forts and fizes, in proportion to the cafes, and to fcrew or fix in the top of the driving block; when you have fixed in a nipple, make, at about 1 ½ inch from it, a fquare hole, in the block, 6 inches deep and 1 inch diameter; then have a piece of wood, 6 inches longer than the cafe intended to be filled, and 2 inches fquare; on 1 fide of it cut a groove almoft the length of the cafe, whofe breadth and depth muft be fufficient to cover near ½ the cafe; then cut the other end to fit the hole in the block, but take care to cut it fo that the groove may be of a proper diftance from the nipple: this half mould being made and fixed tight in the block, cut, in another piece of wood nearly of the fame length as the cafe, a groove of the fame dimenfions as that in the fixed piece; then put the cafe on the nipple, and with a cord tie it and the 2 half moulds together, and your cafe will be ready for filling.

The dimenfions of the above defcribed half moulds, are proportionable for cafes of 8 ounces; but notice muft be taken, that they differ in fize in proportion to the cafes.

Note, the clay, mentioned in this article, muft be prepared after this manner; get fome clay, in which there is no ftones nor fand, and bake it in an oven till quite dry; then take it out and beat it to a powder, and afterwards fift it through a common hair fieve, and it will be fit for ufe.

* A piece of hard wood in the form of an anvil block.

Pro-

Proportion of Mallets.

The best wood for mallets is dry beech. I would have every practitioner know, that if he uses a mallet of a moderate size, in proportion to the rocket, according to his judgement, and if that rocket succeeds, he may depend on the rest, by using the same mallet; yet it will be necessary that cases of different sorts be drove with mallets of different sizes.

The following proportion of the mallets for rockets of any size, from 1 oz. to 6lb. may be observed; but as rockets are seldom made less than 1 oz. or larger than 6lb. I shall leave the management of them to the curious; but all cases under 1 oz. may be rammed with an oz. rocket mallet. Your mallets will strike more solid, by having their handles turned out of the same piece as the head, and made in a cylindrical form: let their dimensions be worked by the diameters of the rockets: for example; let the thickness of the head be 3 diameters, and its length 4, and the length of the handle 5 diameters, whose thickness must be in proportion to the hand.

Proportion of Sky Rockets, and Manner of heading them.

Fig. 13. a rocket compleat without its stick, whose length from the neck is 5 diameters 1-6th; the cases should always be cut to this length after they are filled: M the the head, which is 2 diameters high, and 1 diameter 1-6th ¼ in breadth; N the cone or cap, whose perpendicular height must be 1 diameter 1 3-d. Fig. 14. the collar to which the head is fixed; this is turned out of deal or any light wood, and its exterior diameter must be equal to the interior diameter of the head; 1-6th will be sufficient for its thickness, and round the outside edge must be a groove; the interior diameter of the collar must not be quite so wide as the exterior diameter

of

of the rocket; when this is to be glued on the rocket, you muſt cut 2 or 3 rounds of paper off the caſe, which will make a ſhoulder for it to reſt upon. Fig. 15, a former for the head: 2 or 3 rounds of paper well paſted will be enough for the head, which, when rolled, put the collar on that part of the former marked O, which muſt fit the inſide of it; then, with the pinching cord pinch the bottom of the head into the groove, and tie it with ſmall twine. Fig. 16, a former for the cone. To make the caps, cut your paper in round pieces, equal in diameter to twice the length of the cone you intend to make; which pieces being cut into halves, will make 2 caps each, without waſting any paper; having formed the caps, paſte over each of them a thin white paper, which muſt be a little longer than the cone, ſo as to project about ¼ an inch below the bottom: this projection of paper, being notched and paſted, ſerves to faſten the cap to the head.

When you load the heads of your rockets with ſtars, rains, ſerpents, crackers, ſcrolls, or any thing elſe, accord-ing to your fancy; remember always to put 1 ladle-full of meal powder into each head, which will be enough to burſt the head, and diſperſe the ſtars, or whatever it con-tains: when the heads are loaded with any ſort of caſes, let their mouths be placed downwards; and after the heads are filled, paſte on the top of them a piece of paper, before you put on the caps. As the ſize of ſtars oft differ, it would be needleſs to give an exact number for each rocket, but this rule may be obſerved, that the heads may be nearly filled with whatever they are loaded.

Decorations for Sky Rockets.

Sky rockets bearing the pre-eminence of all fireworks, it will not be improper to treat of their various kinds of decorations, which are directed according to fancy; ſome are headed with ſtars of different ſorts, ſuch as tailed, brilliant, white, blue and yellow ſtars, &c. ſome with gold and ſilver rain; others with ſerpents, crackers, fire-

E   ſcrolls,

scrolls, marrons; and some with small rockets, and many other devices, as the maker pleases.

Dimensions and Poise of Rocket Sticks.

Weight of the rocket.		Length of the stick.		Thickness at top.	Breadth at top.	Square at bottom.	Poise from the point of the cone.	
lb.	oz.	ft.	in.	Inches.	Inches	Inches	ft.	in.
6	0	14	0	1,5	1,85	0,75	4	1,5
4	0	12	10	1,25	1,40	0,625	3	9,
2	0	9	4	1,125	1,	0,525	2	9,
1	0	8	2	0,725	0,80	0,375	2	1,
	8	6	6	0,5	0,70	0,25	1	10,5
	4	5	3	0,3750	0,55	0,35	1	8,5
	2	4	1	0,3	0,45	0,15	1	3,
	1	3	6	0,25	0,35	0,10	11	0,
	$\frac{1}{2}$	2	4	0,125	0,20	0,16	8	0,
	$\frac{1}{4}$	1	$10\frac{1}{2}$	0,1	0,15	0,5	5	0,5

The last column on the right, in the above table, expresses the distance from the top of the cone, where the stick, when tied on, should balance the rocket, so as to stand in an equilibrium on one's finger, or the edge of a knife. The best wood for the sticks is dry deal, made thus; when you have cut and planed the sticks according to the dimensions given in the table, cut on 1 of the flat sides at top, a groove the length of the rocket, and as broad as the stick will allow; then on the opposite flat side, cut 2 notches for the cord, which ties on the rocket, to lay in; 1 of these notches must be near the top of the stick, and the other facing the neck of the rockets; the distance between these notches may easily be known, for the top of the stick should always touch the head of the rocket. When your rockets and sticks are ready, lay the rockets in the grooves in the sticks,

and

and tie them on. Those who, merely for curiosity, may chuse to make rockets of different sizes, to what I have expressed in the table of dimensions, may find the length of their sticks, by making them for rockets, from ½oz. to 1 lb. 60 diameters of the rocket long; and for rockets above 1 lb. 50 or 52 diameters will be a good length; their thickness at top may be about ½ a diameter, and their breadth a very little more; their square at bottom is generally equal to ¼ the thickness at top. But, although the dimensions of the sticks be very nicely observed, you must depend only on their balance : for, without a proper counterpoise, your rockets, instead of mounting perpendicularly, will take an oblique direction, and fall to the ground before they are burnt out.

Boring Rockets which have been drove solid.

Plate 2, Fig. 18, represents the plan of an apparatus, or lathe, for boring of rockets ; A the large wheel which turns the small one B, that works the reammer C : these reammers are of different sizes according to the rockets ; they must be of the same diameter as the top of the bore intended, and continue that thickness a little longer than the depth of the bore required, and their points must be like that of an auger; the thick end of each reammer must be made square, and all of the same size, so as to fit into one socket, wherein they are fastened by a screw D : E the guide for the reammer, which is made to move backwards and forwards ; so that, after you have marked the reammer 3½ diameters of the rocket from the point, set the guide, allowing for the thickness of the fronts of the rocket boxes, and the neck and mouth of the rocket, so that when the front of the large box is close to the guide, the reammer may not go too far up the charge. F, boxes for holding the rockets, which are made so as to fit one in another ; their sides must be equal in thickness to the difference of the diameters of the rockets, and their interior diameters equal to the exterior diameters of the rockets. To prevent the rockets turning round while

boring

boring, a piece of wood muſt be placed againſt the end of the box in the inſide, and preſſed againſt the tail of the rocket; this will alſo hinder the reammer from forcing the rocket backwards. G, a rocket in the box. H, a box that ſlides under the rocket boxes to receive the borings from the rockets, which fall through holes made on purpoſe in the boxes; theſe holes muſt be juſt under the mouth of the rocket, one in each box, and all to correſpond with each other.

Fig. 19, is a front view of the large rocket box. I, an iron plate, in which are holes of different ſizes, through which the reammer paſſes; this plate is faſtened with a ſcrew in the centre, ſo that when you change the reammer, you turn the plate round, but always let the hole you are going to uſe be at the botom : the frents of the other boxes muſt have holes in them to correſpond with them in the plate. K, the lower part of the large box, which is made to fit the inſide of the lathe, that all the boxes may move quite ſteady.

Fig 20, is a perſpective view of the lathe. L, the guide for the reammer, which is ſet by the ſcrew at bottom.

Fig. 21, a view of the front of the guide facing the reammer. M, an iron plate, of the ſame dimenſions as that on the front of the box, and placed in the ſame direction, and alſo to turn on a ſcrew in the centre. N, the rocket box, which ſlides backwards and forwards: when you have fixed a rocket in the box, puſh it forwards againſt the reammer; and when you think the ſcoop of the reammer is full, draw the box back, and knock out the compoſition; this you muſt do till the rocket is bored, or it will be in danger of taking fire; and if you bore in a hurry, wet the end of the reammer now and then with oil to keep it cool.

Having bored a number of rockets, you muſt have taps of different ſorts according to the rockets. Theſe taps are a little longer than the bore, but when you uſe them mark them 3 ½ diameters from the point, allowing for the thickneſs of the rocket's neck; then, holding

the

the rocket in one hand, you tap it with the other. To explain these taps, I have reprefented 1 by Fig. 22. They are made in the fame proportion as the fixed piercers, and are hollowed their whole length.

Hand Machine ufed for boring of Rockets inftead of a Lathe.

Thefe fort of machines anfwer very well, but not fo expeditious as the lathe, nor are they fo expenfive to make; they may be worked by 1 man; but the lathe will require 3. Fig. 23, reprefents the machine. O, the rocket boxes, which are to be fixed, and not to flide as thofe in the lathe. P Q are guides for the reammers, that are made to flide together, as the reammer moves forward: the reammers for thefe fort of machines muft be made of a proper length, allowing for the thicknefs of the front of the boxes, and the length of the mouth and neck of the cafe: on the fquare end of thefe reammers, muft be a round fhoulder of iron, to turn againft the outfide of the guide Q, by which means the guides are forced forwards. R, the ftock which turns the reammer, and while turning muft be preffed towards the the rocket, by the body of the man who works it; all the reammers are to be made to fit 1 ftock. This machine as well as the lathe is made by the fcale in the fame place.

To make large Gerbes.

Fig. 24, reprefents a wooden former; 25, a gerbe complete, with its foot or ftand. The cafes for gerbes are made very ftrong, on account of the ftrength of the compofition; which, when fired, comes out with great velocity; therefore, to prevent their burfting, the paper fhould be pafted, and the cafes made as thick at the top as at the bottom; they fhould alfo have very long necks, for this reafon; firft, that the particles of iron will have more time to be heated, by meeting with greater refift-

ance

in getting out, than with a short neck, which would be burnt too wide before the charge be confumed, and spoil the effect: Secondly, that with long necks the stars will be thrown to a great height, and will not fall before they are spent, or spread too much; but, when made to perfection will rife and spread in such a manner as to form exactly a wheat-sheaf.

In the ramming of gerbes, there will be no need of a mould, the cafes being fufficiently strong to support themfelves; but you are to be careful, before you begin to ram, to have a piece of wood made to fit in the neck; for if this be not done, the compofition will fall into the nec, and leave a vacancy in the cafe, which, as I faid before, will caufe the cafe to burft fo foon as the fire arrives at the vacancy: you muft likewife obferve, that the firft ladle of charge, or 2, if you think proper, be of fome weak compofition. When the cafe is filled, take out the piece of wood, and fill the neck with fome flow charge. Gerbes are generally made about fix diameters long, from the bottom to the top of the neck; their bore muft be 1-5th narrower at top than at bottom. The neck S is 1-6th diameter and $\frac{3}{4}$ long. T, a wooden foot or ftand, on which the gerbe is fixed. This may be made with a choak or cylinder, 4 or 5 inches long, to fit the infide of the cafe, or with a hole in it to put in the gerbe; both thefe methods will anfwer the fame. Gerbes produce a moft brilliant fire, and are very beautiful when a number of them are fixed in the front of a building, or a collection of fireworks.

N. B. Gerbes are made by their diameters, and their cafes at bottom $\frac{1}{4}$ thick. The method of finding the interior diameter of a gerbe is thus: Suppofing you would have the exterior diameter of the cafe, when made, to be 5 inches, then, by taking 2-4ths for the fides of the cafe, there will remain 2 $\frac{1}{2}$ inches for the bore, which will be a very good fize. Thefe fort of gerbes fhould be rammed very hard.

Small

Small Gerbes, or White Fountains,

May be made of 4, 8 oz. or 1 lb. cafes, pafted and made very ftrong, of what length you pleafe; but, before you fill them, drive in dry clay 1 diameter of their orifice high; and, when you have filled a cafe, bore a vent through the centre of the clay to the compofition; the common proportion will do for the vent, which muft be primed with a flow charge. Thefe fort of cafes, without the clay, may be filled with Chinefe fire.

To make Pafte-board and Paper Mortars.

Fig. 26, a former, and 27, an elm foot for the mortar; 28, a mortar complete; thefe mortars are beft when made with pafteboard, well pafted before you begin; or, inftead of pafte, you may ufe glue. For a coehorn mortar, which is 4 inches 2-5ths diameter, roll the pafteboard on the former 1-6th of its diameter thick; and, when dry, cut one end fmooth and even; then nail and glue it on the upper part of the foot; when done, cut off the pafte-board at top, allowing for the length of the mortar 2½ diameters from the mouth of the powder chamber; then bind the mortar round with a ftrong cord wetted with glue. U, the bottom part of the foot, is 1 diameter 2-3ds broad, and 1 diameter high; and that part which goes into the mortar is 2-3ds of its diameter high. W, is a copper chamber for powder, made in a conical form, and is 1-3d of the diameter wide, 1½ of its own diameter long; in the centre of the bottom of this chamber, make a fmall hole a little way down the foot; this hole muft be met by another of the fame fize, made in the fide of the foot, as is fhewn in Fig. 28. If thefe holes are made true, and a copper pipe fitted into both, the mortar when loaded will prime itfelf, for the powder will naturally fall to the bottom of the firft hole; then by putting a bit of quick-match in the fide hole, your mortar will be ready to be fired.

E 4

Mortars

Mortars of 5 ½, 8, and 10 inches diameter, may be made of paper, or pafte-board, by the above method, and in the fame proportion; but if larger, it will be beft to have them made of brafs. N. B. The copper chamber muft have a fmall rim round its edge with holes in it, for fcrews to make it faft in the foot.

SECT. IV.—To load Air Ballóóns, with the Number of Stars, Serpents, Snakes, Rain-falls, &c. in Shells of each Nature.

BALLOONS being in great efteem, by admirers of fire works, I fhall give a full defcription of them.

When you fill your fhells, you muft firft put in the ferpents, rains, ftars, &c. or whatever they are compofed of; then the blowing powder; but the fhells muft not be quite filled; all thofe things muft be put in at the fuze hole; but marrons, being too large to go in at the fuze hole, muft be put in before the infide fhell be joined. When the fhells are loaded, glue and drive in the fuzes very tight. Of thefe fuzes we fhall fay more hereafter; but fhall here give the diameter of the fuze hole in ballóóns of each nature, which are,—For a coehorn ballóón, let the diameter of the fuze hole be 7-8ths of an inch. For a royal ballóón, which is near 5 ¼ inches diameter, make the fuze hole 1 inch 1-8th diameter. For an 8-inch ballóón, 1 inch 3-8ths: and for a 10-inch ballóón, 1 inch 5-8ths.

Having proceeded thus far with the directions of loading ballóóns, I fhall in the fecond place give an account of the quantities and number of each article proper for fhells of each nature; but it is to be obferved, that air-ballóóns are divided into 4 forts, viz. firft, illuminated ballóóns; fecond, ballóóns of ferpents; third, ballóóns

of

of reports, marrons, and crackers; and fourth, compound ballóóns.

Coehorn Ballóón illuminated.

			oz.
Meal } powder {	—— —— ——		1½
Corn } {	—— —— ——		0½
Powder for the mortar	—— ——		2

Length of the fuze compofition ¾ of an inch; 1 oz. drove or rolled ftars, as many as will nearly fill the fhell.

Coehorn Ballóón of Serpents.

			oz.
Meal } powder {	—— —— ——		1½
Corn } {	—— ——		1
Powder for the mortar	—— —— ——		2¼

Length of the fuze compofition 13 16ths of an inch. ½ oz. cafes drove 3 diameters and bounced 3 diameters; and ½ oz. cafes drove 2 diameters and bounced 4; of each an equal quantity, and as many of them as will fit in eafily, placed head to tail.

Coehorn Ballóón of Crackers and Reports.

			oz.
Meal } powder {	—— ——		1¼
Corn } {	—— ——		0¼
Powder for the mortar	——		2

Length of the fuze compofition ¾ of an inch. Reports 4, and crackers of 6 bounces, as many as will fill the fhell.

Compound

Compound Coehorn Ballóóns.

			oz.	dr.
Meal } powder {	——	——	I	4
Corn } powder {	——	——	0	12
Powder for the mortar	——	——	2	4

Length of the fuze compofition 13 16ths of an inch. ½ oz. cafes drove 3 ½ diameters and bounced 2, fixteen; ½ oz. cafes drove 4 diameters and not bounced, 10. Blue ftrung ftars, 10. Rolled ftars as many as will complete the ballóón.

Royal Ballóóns illuminated.

			oz.	dr.
Meal } powder {	——	——	1	8
Corn } powder {	——	——	0	12
Powder for the mortar	——	——	3	0

Length of the fuze compofition 15 16ths of an inch. 2 oz. ftrung ftars, 54: Rolled ftars as many as the fhell will contain, allowing room for the fuze.

Royal Ballóóns of Serpents.

			oz.	dr.
Meal } powder {	——	——	1	0
Corn } powder {	——	——	1	8
Powder for the mortar	——	——	3	8

Length of the fuze compofition 1 inch. 1 oz. cafes drove 3 ½ and 4 diameters, and bounced 2, of each an equal quantity, fufficient to load the fhell.

Royal

Royal Ballóóns with Crackers and Marrons.

					oz.	dr.
Meal } powder {		———	———		1	8
Corn }		———	———		1	4
Powder for firing the mortar		———			3	0

Length of the fuze compofition 14 16ths of an inch; reports 12, and completed with crackers of 8 bounces.

Compound Royal Ballóóns.

					oz.	dr.
Meal } Powder {		———	•		1	5
Corn }		———	———		1	6
Powder for the mortar		———			3	12

Length of the fuze compofition 1 inch. ¼ oz. cafes drove and bounced 2 diameters, 8. 2 ounce cafes filled 3-8ths of an inch with ftar compofition, and bounced 2 diameters, 8. Silver rain-falls, 10. 2 oz. tailed ftars, 16. Rolled brilliant ftars, 30. If this fhould not be fufficient to load the fhell, you may complete it with gold rain-falls.

Eight-inch Ballóóns illuminated.

					oz.	dr.
Meal } powder {		———	———		2	8
Corn }		———	———		1	4
Powder for the mortar		———			9	0

Length of the fuze compofition 1 inch 1 8th. 2 oz. drove ftars, 48. 4 oz. cafes drove with ftar compofition 3 8ths of an inch, and bounced 3 diameters, 12; and the ballóón completed with 2 oz. drove brilliant ftars.

Eight

Eight-inch Ballóóns of Serpents.

			oz.	dr.
Meal } powder {	———	——	2	0
Corn }	———	———	2	0
Powder for the mortar	———	—	9	8

Length of the fuze compofition 1 inch 3 16ths. 2 oz. cafes drove 1¼ diameter, and bounced 2; and 1 oz. cafes drove 2 diameters, and bounced 2½; of each an equal quantity, fufficient for the fhell.

N. B. The ftar compofition drove in bounced cafes, muft be managed thus; firft, the cafes muft be pinched clofe at 1 end, then the corn powder put in for a report, and the cafe pinched again clofe to the powder, only leaving a fmall vent for the ftar compofition, which is drove at top, to communicate to the powder at the bounce end.

REMARKS.

Ballóóns filled with crackers, reports, and marrons, make no great fhow of themfelves, nor are they very pleafing to the eye, for they reprefent nothing more than a number of pale white flafhes, followed by a variety of reports; which all together make but a very indifferent appearance, when fired with illuminated ballóóns, which are fo beautiful and brilliant, as to give fuch luftre as will dazzle the eyes of the fpectators for fome time. On this confideration, I do not think it worth while loading fhells of a large nature with things that afford fo little pleafure; but they have a pretty good effect in royal fhells, when thrown among a number of air works, fuch as pots des brins or flights of rockets, in order to alarm the people with a thundering in the air. For they will not know from whence the reports came, if fired exactly at the fame time with the other works, and the fuze made to carry a fmall fire. But if any one thinks proper to

make

make large ballóóns of this fort, it is only obferving a proportion of the blowing and firing powder, and the length of the fuze, for fhells of the fame dimenfions as thofe you intend to make. Thefe kind of ballóóns are lighter than any other, by reafon of the crackers being light, and not lying clofe in the fhells. It muft be obferved, when you fire light ballóóns, not to put fo much powder in the mortar as for heavy.

Compound 8-inch Ballóóns.

			oz.	dr.
Meal } powder {	——	——	2	8
Corn } powder {	——	——	1	12
Powder for the mortar	——	——	9	4

Length of the fuze compofition 1-8th. 4 oz. cafes drove with ftar compofition 3-8ths of an inch, and bounced 3 diameters, 16. 2 oz. tailed ftars, 16. 2 oz drove brilliant ftars, 12. Silver rain-falls, 20. 1 oz. drove blue ftars, 20: and 1 oz. cafes drove and bounced 2 diameters, as many as will fill the fhell.

Another of 8 inches.

			oz.	dr.
Meal } powder {	——	——	2	8
Corn } powder {	——	——	1	12
Powder for the mortar	——	——	9	4

Length of the fuze compofition 1 inch 1 8th; crackers of 6 reports, 10. Gold rains, 14. 2 oz. cafes drove with ftar compofition 3 8ths of an inch, and bounced 2 diameters, 16. 2 oz. tailed ftars, 16. 2 oz. drove brilliant ftars, 12. Silver rains, 10. 1 oz. drove blue ftars, 20: and 1 oz. cafes drove with a brilliant charge 2 diameters and bounced 3, as many as the fhell will hold.

Another.

Another of 8 inches.

			oz.	dr.
Meal } powder {			2	12
Corn }			2	0
Powder for the mortar			9	0

Length of the fuze compofition 1 inch 1 16th. Crackers of 6 reports, 10. Gold rains, 20. 2 oz. cafes drove with ftar compofition ½ an inch, and bounced 2 diameters, 16. 2 oz. drove brilliant ftars, 2 oz. drove blue ftars, 2 oz. drove coloured ftars, 2 oz drove tailed ftars, large ftrung ftars, and rolled ftars, of each an equal quantity, fufficient for the balloon.

A compound 10-inch Balloón.

			oz.	dr.
Meal } powder {			3	4
Corn }			2	8
Powder for the mortar			12	8

Length of the fuze compofition 15 16ths of an inch. 1 oz. cafes drove and bounced 3 diameters, 16. Crackers of 8 reports, 12. 4 oz. cafes drove ½ an inch with ftar compofition, and bounced 2 diameters, 14. 2 oz. cafes drove with brilliant fire 1 ¼ diameter, and bounced 2 diameters, 16. 2 oz. drove brilliant ftars, 30. 2 oz. drove blue ftars, 30. Gold rains, 20. Silver rains 20. After all thefe are put in, fill the remainder of the cafe with tailed and rolled ftars.

Ten-inch Balloón of 3 changes.

			oz.	dr.
Meal } powder }			3	0
Corn }			3	8
Powder for the mortar			13	0
			Length	

Length of the fuze compofition 1 inch. The fhell muft be loaded with 2 oz. cafes, drove with ftar compofition ¼ of an inch, and on that 1 diameter of gold fire, then bounced 3 diameters; or with 2 oz. cafes firft filled 1 diameter with gold-fire, then ¼ of an inch with ftar compofition, and on that 1 diameter and ½ of brilliant fire. Thefe cafes muft be well fecured at top of the charge, left they fhould take fire at both ends; but their necks muft be larger than the common proportion.

To make Ballóón Fuzes.

Fuzes for air ballóóns are fometimes turned out of dry beech, with a cup at top, to hold the quick-match, as you fee in Plate II. Fig. 28, but if made with pafted paper, they will do as well: the diameter of the former for fuzes for coehorn ballóóns, muft be ½ an inch; for a royal fuze, 5 8ths of an inch; for an 8-inch fuze, ¾ of an inch; and for a 10-inch fuze, 7 8ths of an inch. Having rolled your cafes, pinch and tie them almoft clofe at one end; then drive them down, and let them dry; before you begin to fill them, mark, on the outfide of the cafe, the length of charge required, allowing for the thicknefs of the bottom; and when you have rammed in the compofition, take 2 pieces of quick-match, about 6 inches long, and lay one end of each on the charge, and then a little meal powder, which ram down hard; the loofe ends of the match double up into the top of the fuze, and cover it with a paper cap to keep it dry. When you put the fhells in the mortars, uncap the fuzes, and pull out the loofe ends of the match, and let them hang on the fides of the ballóóns. The ufe of the match is, to receive the fire rom the powder in the chamber of the mortar, in order to light the fuze: the fhell being put in the mortar with the fuze uppermoft, and exactly in the centre; fprinkle over it a little meal-powder, and it will be ready to be fired. Fuzes made of wood muft be longer than thofe of paper, and not bored quite through, but left folid about ¼ an inch at bottom; and

when

when you use them, saw them off to a proper length, mea-
suring the charge from the cup at top.

Tourbillons.

Having filled some cases within about 1 ¼ diameter,
drive in a ladle-full of clay, then pinch their ends close,
and drive them down with a mallet; when done, find
the centre of gravity of each case, where you nail and
tie a stick, which should be ⅝ an inch broad at the middle, and run a little narrower to the ends: these sticks
must have their ends turned upwards, so that the cases
may turn horizontally on their centres: at the opposite
sides of the cases, at each end, bore a hole close to the
clay with a gimblet, the size of the neck of a common
case of the same nature; from these holes draw a line
round the case, and at the under part of the case bore a
hole, with the same gimblet, within ⅛ a diameter of each
line towards the centre, then from one hole to the other
draw a right line. This line divide into 3 equal parts,
and at X and Y, Fig. 29, Plate III. bore a hole, then
from these holes to the other 2, lead a quick-match, over
which paste a thin paper. Fig. 30 represents a tourbillon as it should lie to be fired, with a leader from one
side hole A, to the other B. When you fire tourbillons,
lay them on a smooth table, with their sticks downwards,
and burn the leader through the middle with a port fire.
They should spin 3 or 4 seconds on the table before
they rise, which is about the time the composition will
be burning, from the side holes to those at bottom.

To tourbillons may be fixed reports, in this manner:
in the centre of the case at top, make a small hole, and
in the middle of the report make another; then place
them together, and tie on the report, and with a single
paper secure it from fire: this done, your tourbillon is com-
pleated. By this method you may fix on tourbillons,
small cones of stars, rains, &c. but be careful not to load
them too much. 18th of an inch will be enough for
the thickness of the sticks, and their length equal to that
of the cases.

To

To make Mortars to throw Aigrettes, and to load and fire them.

Mortars to throw aigrettes are generally made of pafte-board, of the fame thicknefs as ballóon mortars, and 2 ¼ diameters long in the infide from the top of the foot: the foot muſt be made of elm without a chamber, but flat at top, and in the fame proportion as thofe for bal-loon mortars; thefe mortars muſt alfo be bound round with cord as before mentioned: fometimes 8 or 9 of thefe mortars, of about 3 or 4 inches diameter, are bound all together fo as to appear but 1; but when they are made for this purpofe, the bottom of the foot muſt be of the fame diameter as the mortars, and only ⅓ a dia-meter high. Your mortars being bound well together, fix them on a heavy folid block of wood: to load thefe mortars, firſt put on the infide bottom of each, a piece of paper, and on it fpread 1 ¼ oz. of meal and corn powder mixed; then tie your ferpents up in parcels with quick-match, and put them in the mortar with their mouths downwards; but take care the parcels do not fit too tight in the mortars, and that all the ferpents have been well primed with powder wetted with fpirit of wine: on the top of the ferpents in each mortar lay fome paper or tow; then carry a leader from one mortar to the other all round, and then from all the outfide mortars into that in the middle: thefe leaders muſt be put be-tween the cafes and the fides of the mortar, down to the powder at bottom: in the centre of the middle mortar fix a fire-pump, or brilliant fountain, which muſt be open at bottom, and long enough to project out of the mouth of the mortar; then pafte paper on the tops of all the mortars.

Mortars thus prepared are called a Neſt of Serpents, as reprefented by Fig. 31. When you would fire thefe mortars, light the fire-pump C, which when confumed will communicate to all the mortars at once, by means of the leaders. For mortars of 6, 8, or 10 inches dia-

F　　　　meter,

meter, the ferpents fhould be made in 1 and 2 oz. cafes, 6 or 7 inches long, and fired by a leader, brought out of the mouth of the mortar, and turned down the outfide, and the end of it covered with paper, to prevent the fparks of the other works from fetting it on fire. For a 6 inch mortar, let the quantity of powder for firing be 2 oz. for an 8-inch, 2 ¾ oz. and for a 10 inch, 3 ½ oz. Care muft be taken in thefe, as well as fmall mortars, not to put the ferpents in too tight, for fear of burfing the mortars. Thefe mortars may be loaded with ftar, crackers, &c.

If the mortars, when loaded, are to be fent any diftance, or liable to be much moved, the firing powder fhould be fecured from getting amongft the ferpents, which would endanger the mortars, as well as hurt their performance ; to prevent which, load your mortars thus : firft put in the firing powder, and fpread it equally about ; then cut a round piece of blue touch-paper, equal to the exterior diameter of the mortar, and draw on it a circle, equal to the interior diameter of the mortar, and notch it all round as far as that circle ; then pafte that part which is notched, and put it down the mortar clofe to the powder, and ftick the pafted edge to the mortar : this will keep the powder always fmooth at bottom, fo that it may be moved or carried any where, without receiving damage. The large fingle mortars are called Pots des Aigrettes.

Making, loading, and firing of Pots des Brins.

Thefe are made of pafte-board, and muft be rolled pretty thick ; ufually made 3 or 4 inches diameter, and 4 diameters long, and pinched with a neck at one end, like common cafes. A number of thefe are placed on a plank thus : having fixed on a plank 2 rows of wooden pegs, cut, in the bottom of the plank, a groove the whole length under each row of pegs ; then, through the centre of each peg, bore a hole down to the groove at bottom, and on every peg fix and glue a pot, whofe mouth muft fit tight on the peg: through all the holes run a quick-match, one end of which muft go into the pot, and the other into the groove, which muft have a match laid in it from end to end, and covered with paper, fo that when lighted at one end, it may difcharge the whole almoft inftantaneoufly: in all the pots put about 1 oz. of meal and corn powder; then in fome put ftars, and others rains, fnakes, ferpents, crackers, &c. when they are all loaded, pafte paper over their mouths. 2 or 300 of thefe pots being fired together, make a very pretty fhow, by affording fo great a variety of fires. Fig. 32 is a range of pots des brins, with the leader A, by which they are fired.

Pots des Sauciffons

Are generally fired out of large mortars without chambers, the fame as thofe for aigrettes, only fomewhat ftronger: fauciffons are made of 1 and 2 oz. cafes, 5 or 6 inches long, and choaked in the fame maner as ferpents: half the number which the mortar contains, muft be drove 1 ¼ diameter with compofition, and the other half 2 diameters, fo that when fired they may give 2 volleys of reports; but if the mortars are very ftrong, and will bear a fufficient charge, to throw the fauciffons very high, you may make 3 volleys of reports, by dividing the number of cafes into 3 parts, and making a difference in the height of the charge: after they are filled, pinch and tie them at top of the charge, almoft clofe; only leaving a fmall vent to communicate the fire to the upper part of the cafe, which muft be filled with corn powder very near the top; then pinch the end quite clofe, and tie it; after this is done, bind the cafe very tight with waxed pack-thread, from the choak at top of the compofition, to the end of the cafe; this will make the cafe very ftrong in that part, and caufe the report to be very loud: fauciffons fhould be rolled a little thicker of paper than the common proportion. When they are to be put in the mortar, they muft be primed in their mouths, and fired by a cafe of brilliant fire fixed in their centre.

The charge for thefe mortars fhould be 1-6th, or 1-8th, more than for pots des aigrettes of the fame diameter.

To fix one Rocket on the Top of another.

When fky rockets are thus managed, they are called Towering Rockets, on account of their mounting fo very high. Towering rockets are made after this manner; fix on a pound rocket a head without a collar; then take a oz. rocket, which may be headed or bounced, and rub the mouth of it with meal powder wetted with fpirit of wine; when done, put it in the head of the large rocket with its mouth downwards; but before you put it in, ftick a bit of quick-match in the hole in the clay of the pound rocket, which match fhould be long enough to go a little way up the bore of the fmall rocket, to fire it, when the large is burnt out: the 4 oz. rocket being too fmall to fill the head of the other, roll round it as much tow as will make it ftand upright in the centre of the head: the rocket being thus fixed, pafte a fingle paper round the opening of the top of the head of the large rocket. The large rocket muft have only half a diameter of charge rammed above the piercer, for, if filled to the ufual height, it would turn before the fmall one takes fire, and entirely deftroy the intended effect: when one rocket is headed with another, there will be no occafion for any blowing powder; for the force with which it fets off, will be fufficient to difengage it from the head of the firft fired rocket. The fticks for thefe rockets muft be a little longer than for thofe headed with ftars, rains, &c.

Caduceus Rockets,

In rifing, form 2 fpiral lines, or double worm, by rea-fon of their being placed obliquely, one oppofite the other;

other; and their counterpoise in their centre, which causes them to rise in a vertical direction. Rockets for this purpose must have their ends choaked close, without either head or bounce; for a weight at top would be a great obstruction to their mounting; though I have known them sometimes to be bounced, but then they did not rise so high as those that were not; nor do any Caduceus rockets ascend so high as single, because of their serpentine motion, and likewise the resistance of air, which is much greater than 2 rockets of the same size would meet with, if fired singly.

By Fig. 33. you see the method of fixing these rockets: the sticks for this purpose must have all their sides equal, which sides should be equal to the breadth of a stick proper for a sky rocket of the same weight as those you intend to use, and to taper downwards as usual, long enough to balance them, 1 length of a rocket, from the cross stick; which must be placed from the large stick, 6 diameters of 1 of the rockets, and its length 7 diameters; so that each rocket, when tied on, may form with the large stick an angle of 60 degrees. In tying on the rockets, place their heads on the opposite sides of the cross stick, and their ends on the opposite sides of the long stick; then carry a leader from the mouth of one into that of the other. When these rockets are to be fired, suspend them between 2 hooks or nails, then burn the leader through the middle, and both will take fire at the same time. Rockets of 1 lb. are a good size for this use.

Honorary Rockets

Are the same as sky rockets, except that they carry no head nor report, but are closed at top, on which is fixed a cone; then on the case, close to the top of the stick, you tie a 2 oz. case, about 5 or 6 inches long, filled with a strong charge, and pinched close at both ends; then in the reverse sides, at each end, bore a hole in the same manner as in tourbillons; from each hole carry a

leader

leader into the top of the rocket. When the rocket is fired, and arrived to its proper height, it will give fire to the cafe at top, which will caufe both rocket and ftick to fpin very faft in their return, and reprefent a worm of fire, defcending to the ground.

There is another method of placing the fmall cafe, which is by letting the ftick rife a little above the top of the rocket, and tying the cafe to it, fo as to reft on the rocket: thefe rockets have no cones.

There is alfo a third method, by which they are managed, which is thus: in the top of a rocket fix a piece of wood, in which drive a fmall iron fpindle; then make a hole in the middle of the fmall cafe, through which put the fpindle; then fix on the top of it a nut, to keep the cafe from falling off; when this is done, the cafe will turn very faft, without the rocket: but this method does not anfwer fo well as either of the former.

Fig. 34. is the honorary rocket complete. The beft fized rockets for this purpofe are thofe of 1lb.

To divide the Tail of a Sky Rocket fo as to form an Arch when afcending.

Having fome rockets made, and headed according to fancy, and tied on their fticks; get fome fheet tin, and cut it into round pieces about 3 or 4 inches diameter; then on the ftick of each rocket, under the mouth of the cafe, fix 1 of thefe pieces of tin, 16 inches from the rocket's neck, and fupport it by a wooden bracket, as ftrong as poffible: the ufe of this is, that when the rocket is afcending, the fire will play with great force on the tin, which will divide the tail in fuch a manner, that it will form an arch as it mounts, and will have a very good effect when well managed: if there is a fhort piece of port-fire, of a ftrong charge, tied to the end of the ftick, it will make a great addition; but this muft be lighted before you fire the rocket.

To

To make several Sky Rockets rise in the same direction, and equally distant from each other.

Take 6 or any number of sky rockets, of what size you please; then cut some strong pack-thread into pieces of 3 or 4 yards long, and tie each end of these pieces to a rocket in this manner. Having tied one end of your pack-thread round the body of one rocket, and the other end to another; take a 2nd piece of pack-thread and make one end of it fast to one of the rockets already tied, and the other end to a 3d rocket, so that all the rockets, except the 2 outside, will be fastened to 2 pieces of pack-thread: the length of thread from one rocket to the other, may be what the maker pleases; but the rockets must be all of a size, and their heads filled with the same weight of stars, rains, &c.

Having thus done, fix in the mouth of each rocket a leader of the same length; and, when you are going to fire them, hang them almost close; then tie the ends of the leaders together, and prime them: this prime being fired, all the rockets will mount at the same time, and divide as far as the strings will allow; which division they will keep, provided they are all rammed alike, and well made. They are called, by some, Chained Rockets.

Signal Sky Rockets

Are made of several kinds, according to the different signals intended to be given: but in Artificial Fireworks, 2 sorts are only used, which are one with reports, and the other without; but those for the use of the Navy and Army are headed with stars, serpents, &c.——Rockets which are to be bounced, must have their cases made 1 ½ or 2 diameters longer than the common proportion,

and

and, after they are filled, drive in a double quantity of clay; then bounce and pinch them, after the ufual man- ner, and fix on each a cap.

Signal fky rockets without bounces, are only fky rockets clofed and capped: thefe are very light, therefore do not require fuch heavy fticks as thofe with loaded heads; for which reafon, you may cut one length of the rocket off the ftick, or elfe make them thinner.

Signal rockets with reports, are fired in fmall flights; and oft both thefe, and thofe without reports, are ufed for a fignal to begin firing a collection of works.

To fix two or more Sky Rockets on one ftick.

Two, 3, or 6 fky rockets, fixed on 1 ftick, and fired together, make a grand and beautiful appearance; for the tails of all will feem but as one of an immenfe fize, and the breaking of fo many heads at once will re- femble the burfting of an air balloon; but the manage- ment of this device requires a fkilful hand; therefore, for the encouragement of thofe who are fond of curious performances, I fhall give fuch inftructions, that, if well obferved, even by thofe who have not made a great progrefs in this art, there will be no doubt of the rockets having the defired effect.

Rockets for this purpofe muft be made with the greateft exactnefs, all rammed by the fame hand, in the fame mould, and out of the one proportion of com- pofition; and after they are filled and headed, muft all be of the fame weight: the ftick muft alfo be well made, (and proportioned) to the following directions: firft, fup- pofing your rockets to be ½ pounders, whofe fticks are 6 feet 6 inches long, then if 2, 3, or 6 of thefe are to be fixed on 1 ftick, let the length of it be 9 feet 9 inches; then cut the top of it into as many fides, as there are rockets, and let the length of each fide be equal to the length of 1 of the rockets without its head; and in each fide cut a groove, (as ufual); then from the grooves

plane

plane it round, down to the bottom, where its thickness muſt be equal to half the top of the round part. As their thickneſs cannot be exactly aſcertained, I ſhall give a rule which generally anſwers for any number of rockets above two : the rule is this; that the ſtick at top muſt be thick enough, when the grooves are cut, for all the rockets to lie, without preſſing each other, though as near as poſſible.

When only 2 rockets are to be fixed on 1 ſtick, let the length of the ſtick be the laſt given proportion, but ſhaped after the common method, and the breadth and thickneſs, double the dimenſions given in the Table, page 50. The point of poiſe muſt be in the uſual place, (let the number of rockets be what they will :) if ſticks made by the above directions ſhould be too heavy, plane them thinner; and if too light, make them thicker; but always make them of the ſame length.

When more than two rockets are tied on one ſtick, there will be ſome danger of their flying up without the ſtick, unleſs the following precaution is taken ; for caſes being placed on all ſides, there can be no notches for the cord which ties on the rockets to lie in ; therefore, inſtead of notches, drive a ſmall nail, in each ſide of the ſtick, between the necks of the caſes ; and let the cord, which goes round their necks, be brought cloſe under the nails; by this means the rockets will be as ſecure, as when tied on ſingly. Your rockets being thus fixed, carry a quick-match, without a pipe, from the mouth of one rocket to the other; this match being lighted will give fire to all at once.

Though the directions already given may be ſufficient for theſe rockets, I ſhall here add an improvement of my own, on a very eſſential part of this device, which is, that of hanging the rockets to be fired; for before I hit upon the following method, many of my eſſays proved unſucceſsful ; but to prevent ſuch perplexities, inſtead of the old and common manner of hanging them on nails or hooks, make uſe of this contrivance : have a ring made of ſtrong iron wire, large

enough

enough for the stick to go in, as far as the mouths of the rockets ; then let this ring be supported by a small iron, at some distance from the post or stand to which it is fixed ; then have another ring, fit to receive and guide the small end of the stick. Rockets thus suspended will have nothing to obstruct their fire ; but when they are hung on nails or hooks, in such a manner, that some of their mouths are against or upon a rail, there can be no certainty of their rising in a vertical direction.

To fire Sky-rockets without Sticks.

You must have a stand, of a block of wood, a foot diameter, and make the bottom flat, so that it may stand steady ; in the centre of the top of this block draw a circle 2 ½ inches diameter, and divide the circumference of it into 3 = parts ; then take 3 pieces of thick iron wire, each about 3 feet long, and drive them into the block, 1 at each point made on the circle ; when these wires are drove in deep enough to hold them fast, and upright, so that the distance from one to the other is the same at top as at bottom, the stand is complete.

The stand being thus made, prepare your rockets thus : take some common sky-rockets, of any size, and head them as you please ; then get some balls of lead, and tie to each a small wire, 2 or 2 ½ feet long, and the other end of each wire tie to the neck of a rocket : these balls answer the purpose of sticks, when made of a proper weight, which is about 2-3ds the weight of the rocket ; but when they are of a proper size, they will balance the rocket in the same manner as a stick, at the usual point of poise. To fire these, hang them, one at a time, between the tops of the wires, letting their heads rest on the point of the wires, and the balls hang down between them : if the wires should be too wide for the rockets, press them together, till they fit, and if too close, force them open : the wires for this purpose must be softened, so as not to have any spring,

or

or they will not keep their position, when pressed close or opened.

Rain-falls for Sky-rockets, Double and Single.

Gold and silver rain composition are drove in cases that are pinched quite close at one end: if you roll them dry, 4 or 5 rounds of paper will be strong enough, but if they are pasted, 3 rounds will do; and the thin sort of cartridge paper is best for those small cases, which in rolling you must not turn down the inside edge, as in other cases, for a double edge would be too thick for so small a bore. The moulds for rain-falls should be made of brass, and turned very smooth in the inside; or the cases, which are so very thin, would tear in coming out; for the charge must be drove in tight; and the better the case fits the mould, the more driving it will bear. These moulds have no nipple, but instead of which they are made flat: as it would be very tedious and troublesome to shake the composition out of such small ladles, as are used for these cases, it will be necessary to have a funnel, made of thin tin, to fit on the top of the case, by the help of which you may fill them very fast. For single rain-falls for 4 oz. rockets, let the diameter of the former be 2 16ths of an inch, and the length of the case 2 inches; for 8 oz. rockets, 4 16ths, and 2 diameters of the rocket long; for 1lb. rockets, 5 16ths, and 2 diameters of the rocket long; for 2 lb. rockets, 5 16ths, and 3 ½ inches long; for 4 lb. rockets, 6 16ths, and 4 ½ inches long; and for 6-pounders, 7 16ths diameter, and 5 inches long.

Of double rain-falls there are 2 sorts; as, for example, some appear first like a star, and then as rain; and some appear first as rain, and then like a star: when you would have stars first, you must fill the cases, within ½ an inch of the top, with rain composition, and the remainder with star composition; but when you intend the rain should be first, drive the case ½ an inch with star composition,

and

the reft with rain. By this method may be made many changes of fire; for in large rockets you may make them firft burn as ftars, then rain, and again as ftars; or they may firft fhew rain, then ftars, and finifh with a report; but when they are thus managed, cut open the firft-rammed end; after they are filled and bounced, at which place prime them. The ftar compofition for this puipofe muft be a little ftronger than for rolled ftars.

Strung Stars.

Firft take fome thin paper, and cut it into pieces of 1 ½ inch fquare, or thereabouts; then on each piece lay as much dry ftar compofition as you think the paper will eafily contain; then twift up the paper as tight as you can; when done, rub fome pafte on your hands, and roll the ftars between them; then fet them to dry: your ftars being thus made, get fome flax or fine tow, and roll a little of it over each ftar; then pafte your hands and roll the ftars as before, and fet them again to dry; when they are quite dry, with a piercer make a hole through the middle of each, into which run a cotton quick-match, long enough to hold 10 or 12 ftars, at 3 or 4 inches diftance: but any number of ftars may be ftrung together by joining the match,

Tailed Stars.

Thefe are called tailed ftars, becaufe there are a great number of fparks iffue from them, which reprefent a tail like that of a comet. Of thefe there are two forts, which are Rolled and Drove: when rolled, they muft be moiftened with a liquor made of half a pint of fpirit of wine, and half a gill of thin fize, of this as much as will wet the compofition enough to make it roll eafy; when they are rolled, fift meal powder over them, and fet them to dry.

When tailed ftars are drove, the compofition muft be moiftened with fpirit of wine only, and not made fo

wet

wet as for rolling: 1 and 2 oz. cases, rolled dry, are best for this purpose; and when they are filled, unroll the case within 3 or 4 rounds of the charge, and all that you unroll cut off; then paste down the loose edge: 2 or 3 days after the cases are filled, cut them in pieces 5 or 6 8ths of an inch in length; then melt some wax, and dip one end of each piece into it, so as to cover the composition: the other end must be rubbed with meal powder wetted with spirit of wine.

Drove Stars.

Cases for drove stars are rolled with paste, but are made very thin of paper: before you begin to fill them, damp the composition with spirit of wine that has had some camphor dissolved in it; you may ram them indifferently hard, so that you do not break, or sack the case, to prevent which, they should fit tight in the mould: they are drove in cases of several sizes, from 8 drams to 4 oz. when they are filled in ½ oz. cases, cut them in pieces of ¾ of an inch long; if 1 oz. cases, cut them in pieces of 1 inch: if 2 oz. cases, cut them in pieces of 1¼ inch long; and if 4 oz. cases, cut them in pieces of 1½ inch long: having cut your stars of a proper size, prime both ends with wet meal powder. These stars are seldom put in rockets, they being chiefly intended for air balloons, and drove in cases, to prevent the composition from being broke by the force of the blowing powder in the shell.

Rolled Stars

Are commonly made about the size of a musket ball, though they are rolled of several sizes, from the bigness of a pistol ball, to 1 inch diameter; and sometimes very small, but then called sparks. Great care must be taken in making stars first, that the several ingredients are reduced to a fine powder; secondly, that the composition is well worked and mixed. Before you begin to roll, take about a pound of composition, and wet it with the

following

following liquid, enough to make it stick together and roll easy; spirit of wine 1 quart, in which dissolve ¼ of an ounce of isinglass. If a great quantity of composition be wetted at once, the spirit will evaporate, and leave it dry, before you can roll it into stars: having rolled up one proportion, shake the stars in meal powder, and set them to dry, which they will do in 3 or 4 days; but if you should want them for immediate use, dry them in an earthen pan over a slow heat, or in an oven. It being very difficult to make the stars all of an equal size, when the composition is taken up promiscuously with the fingers; therefore I shall here set down a method by which you may make them very exact, which is,—When the mixture is moistened properly, roll it on a flat smooth stone, and cut it into square pieces, making each square large enough for the stars you intend. There is another method used by some to make stars, which is by rolling the composition in long pieces, and then cutting off the star, so that each star will be of a cylindrical form; but this method is not so good as the former, for to make the composition roll this way, it must be made very wet, which makes the stars heavy, as well as weakens them. All stars must be kept as much from air as possible, otherwise they will grow weak and bad.

Scrolls for Sky Rockets.

Cases for scrolls should be made 4 or 5 inches in length, and their interior diameter 3 8ths of an inch: one end of these cases must be pinched quite close, before you begin to fill, and when filled, close the other end; then in the opposite sides make a small hole at each end, to the composition, in the same manner as in Tourbillons; and prime them with wet meal powder. You may put in the head of a rocket as many of these cases as it will contain: being fired they turn very quick in the air, and form a scroll or spiral line. They are generally filled with a strong charge, as that of serpents, or brilliant fire.

Swarmers,

Swarmers, or small Rockets.

Rockets that go under the denomination of Swarmers, are those from 2 oz. downwards. These rockets are fired sometimes in flights, and in large water-works, &c. Swarmers of 1 and 2 oz. are bored, and made in the same manner as large rockets, except, when headed, their heads must be put on without a collar: the number of strokes for driving 1 oz. must be eight; and for 2 oz. twelve.

All rockets under 1 oz. are not bored, but must be filled to the usual height with composition, which is generally composed of fine meal powder 4 oz. and charcoal or steel dust 2 drams: the number of strokes for ramming these small swarmers is not material, so as they are rammed true, and moderately hard. The necks of unbored rockets must be in the same proportion as in common cases.

The cause of Sky Rockets rising.

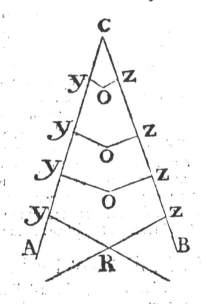

Having promised, in the second section, to prove that the effect of sky rockets, and proportion of their charge, depends on the size of the cavity in the composition; I shall here endeavour to give a mathematical demonstration thereof.

Let

Let ABC be the hollow cone for the fire, AYCZB, the fuperficies of that cone, all the lines OZ at right angles with BC, all the lines OY at right angles with A :̲ now all the angles ZOY being towards R, whether the angles ZOY are obtufe or acute, but the more acute the better. The rays of fire ZO and YO iffuing from the fides of the cone BC and AC, and continually acting with the greater force one upon another at O, forcing the whole BCA upward from the point R; and the wider the cone is, (fo as not to exceed one third at bottom, and one fixth at top, of the exterior diameter of the rocket) the greater velocity will the rocket rife with.

Stands for Sky Rockets.

Care muft be taken, in placing the rockets, when they are to be fired, to give them a vertical direction at their firft fetting out; which may be managed thus. Have 2 rails of wood, of any length, fupported at each end by a perpendicular leg, fo that the rails be horizontal, and let the diftance from one to the other be almoft equal to the length of the fticks of the rockets intended to be fired; then in the front of the top rail drive fquare hooks at 8 inches diftance, with their points turning fideways, fo that when the rockets are hung on them, the points will be before the fticks, and keep them from falling, or being blown off by the wind: in the front of the rail at bottom muft be ftaples, drove perpendicular under the hooks at top; through thefe ftaples put the fmall ends of the rocket fticks. Rockets are fired by applying a lighted port fire to their mouths.

N. B. When fky rockets are made to perfection, and fired, they will ftand 2 or 3 feconds on the hook before they rife, and then mount up brifkly, with a fteady motion, carrying a large tail from the ground all the way up, and, juft as they turn, break and difperfe the ftars.

Girandole Chefts, for flights of Rockets,

Are generally compofed of four fides, of equal dimenfions; but may be made of any diameter, according to

the

the number of rockets defigned to be fired; its height muft be in proportion to the rockets, but muft always be a little higher than the rockets with their fticks. When the fides are joined, fix in the top, as far down the cheft as the length of one of the rockets with its cap on. In this top, make as many fquare or round holes to receive the rocket fticks, as you intend to have rockets; but let the diftance between them be fufficient for the rockets to ftand without touching one another; then from one hole to another cut a groove, large enough for a quick-match to lie in: the top being thus fixed, put in the bottom, at about 1 ½ foot diftance from the bottom of the cheft; in this bottom muft be as many holes as in the top, and all to correfpond; but thefe holes need not be fo large as thofe in the top.

To prepare your cheft, you muft lay a quick-match, in all the grooves, from hole to hole; then take fome fky rocke s, and rub them in the mouth with wet meal powder, and put a bit of match up the cavity of each, which match muft be long enough to hang a little below the mouth of the rocket. Your rockets and cheft being prepared according to the above directions, put the fticks of the rockets through the holes in the top and bottom of the cheft, fo that their mouths may reft on the quick-match in the grooves; by which all the rockets will be fired at once; for by giving fire to any part of the match, it will communicate to all the rockets in an inftant. As it would be rather troublefome to direct the fticks from the top to the proper holes in the bottom, it will be neceffary to have a fmall door in one of the fides, which when opened, you may fee how to place the fticks. Flights of rockets, being feldom fired at the beginning of any fireworks, for which reafon they are in danger of being fired by the fparks from wheels, &c. therefore to preferve them, a cover fhould be made to fit on the cheft, and the door in the fide kept fhut.

G   Serpents

Serpents or Snakes for Pots of Aigrettes, Small Mortars, Sky Rockets, &c.

Serpents for this ufe are made from 2 ¼ inches, to 7 inches long, and their formers from 3 16ths to 5 8ths of an inch diameter; but the diameter of the cafes muſt always be equal to 2 diameters of the former; they are rolled and choaked like other cafes, and filled with compoſition from 5 8ths of an inch, to 1 ¼ inch high, according to the ſize of the mortars, or rockets, they are defigned for, and the remainder of the cafes bounced with corn-powder, and afterwards their ends pinched and tied clofe: before they are ufed, their mouths muſt be primed with wet meal-powder.

Leaders, or Pipes of Communication.

The beſt paper for leaders, is Elephant, which you cut into long flips, 2 or 3 inches broad, fo that they may go 3 or 4 times round the former, but not more : when they are very thick, they are too ſtrong for the paper which faſtens them to the works, and will fometimes fly off without leading the fire. The formers for thefe leaders are made from 2 to 6 16ths of an inch diameter ; but 4 16ths is the ſize generally made ufe of: the formers are made of ſmooth brafs wire: when you ufe them, rub them over with greafe, or keep them wet with paſte, to prevent their ſticking to the paper, which muſt be paſted. all over. In rolling of pipes, make ufe of a rolling-board, but ufe it lightly: having rolled a pipe, draw out the former with one hand, holding the pipe as light as poſſible with the other; for, if it prefs againſt the former, it will ſtick and tear the paper.

N. B. Make your leaders of different lengths, or in clothing of works you will cut a great many to wafte. Leaders for marron batteries muſt be made of ſtrong cartridge paper.

SECT.

SECT. V. Aquatic Fireworks.

WORKS that sport in the water are much esteemed by most admirers of fireworks, particularly water rockets; but, as they seem of a very extraordinary nature to those who are acquainted with this art, I shall endeavour to explain the method of making them, in as full and easy a manner as possible, as well as other devices for the water.

Water Rockets

May be made from 4 oz. to 2 lb. but, if larger, are too heavy; so that it will be difficult to make them keep above water without a cork float, which must be tied to the neck of the case; but the rockets will not dive so well with, as without floats.

Cases for these are made in the same manner and proportion as sky rockets, only a little thicker of paper. When you fill them which are drove solid, put in first 1 ladle-full of slow fire, then 2 of the proper charge and on that 1 or 2 ladles of sinking charge, then the proper charge, then the sinking charge again, and so on, till you have filled the case within 3 diameters; then drive on the composition 1 ladle-full of clay; through which make a small hole to the charge; then fill the case, within $\frac{1}{4}$ a diameter, with corn powder, on which turn down 2 or 3 rounds of the case in the inside; then pinch and tie the end very tight: having filled your rockets, (according to the above directions) dip their ends in melted rosin, or sealing wax, or else secure them well with grease. When you fire these rockets, throw in 6 or 8 at a time; but, if you would have them all sink, or swim, at the same time, you must drive them with an equal quantity of composition, and fire them all together.

To make Pipes of Communication, which may be ufed under Water.

Pipes for this purpofe muft be a little thicker of paper than thofe for land. Having rolled a fufficient number of pipes, and kept them till dry, wafh them over with drying oil, and fet them to dry; but when you oil them, leave about 1½ inch at each end dry, for joints: if they were oiled all over, when you come to join them, the pafte would not ftick where the paper is greafy: after the leaders are joined, and the pafte dry, oil the joints. Thefe pipes will lie many hours under water, without receiving any damage.

Horizontal Wheels for the Water.

Firft get a large wooden bowl without a handle; then have an octagon wheel made of a flat board, 18 inches diameter, fo that the length of each fide will be near 7 inches: in all the fides cut a groove for the cafes to lie in. This wheel being made, nail it on the top of the bowl; then take 8 four-ounce cafes, filled with a proper charge, each about 6 inches in length. Now, to clothe the wheel with thefe cafes, get fome whitifh-brown paper, and cut it into flips 4 or 5 inches broad, and 7 or 8 long: thefe flips being pafted all over on one fide, take 1 of the cafes, and roll 1 of the flips of paper about 1½ inch on its end, fo that there will remain about 2½ inches of the paper hollow from the end of the cafe: this cafe tie on 1 of the fides of the wheel, near the corners of which muft be holes bored, through which you put the pack-thread to tie the cafes: having tied on the firft cafe at the neck and end, put a little meal powder in the hollow paper; then pafte a flip of paper on the end of another cafe, the head of which put into the hollow paper on the firft, allowing a fufficient diftance, from the tail of one to the head of the other, for the pafted paper to bend without tearing: the fecond cafe tie on as you did the

firft;

firſt; and ſo on with the reſt, except the laſt, which
muſt be cloſed at the end, unleſs it is to communicate to
any thing on top of the wheel; ſuch as fire-pumps or
brilliant fires, fixed in holes, cut in the wheel, and fired
by the laſt or ſecond caſe, as the fancy directs: 6, 8, or
any number, may be placed on the top of the wheel, ſo
that they are not too heavy for the bowl.

Before you tie on the caſes, cut the upper part of all
their ends, except the laſt, a little ſhelving, that the fire
from one may play over the other, without being ob-
ſtructed by the caſe. Wheel caſes have no clay drove
in their ends, nor pinched, but are always left open,
only the laſt, or thoſe which are not to lead fire, which
muſt be well ſecured.

Water Mines.

For theſe mines you muſt have a bowl, with a wheel
on it, made in the ſame manner as the water wheel, only
in its middle muſt be a hole, of the ſame diameter you
deſign to have the mine. Theſe mines are tin pots, with
ſtrong bottoms, and a little more than 2 diameters in
length: your mine muſt be fixed in the hole in the wheel,
with its bottom reſting on the bowl; then loaded with
ſerpents, crackers, ſtars, ſmall water rockets, &c. in
the ſame manner as pots of aigrettes; but in their centre fix a caſe of Chineſe fire, or a ſmall gerbe, which
muſt be lighted at the beginning of the laſt caſe on the
wheel. Theſe wheels are to be clothed as uſual.

Fire Globes for the Water.

Bowls for water globes muſt be very large, and the
wheels on them of a decagon form; on each ſide of
which nail a piece of wood 4 inches long, and on the
outſide of each piece cut a groove, wide enough to receive about ¼ of the thickneſs of a 4 oz. caſe: theſe
pieces of wood muſt be nailed in the middle of each face
of the wheel, and fixed in an oblique direction, ſo that
the fire from the caſes may incline upwards: the wheel

G 3 being

being thus prepared, tie in each groove a 4 oz. cafe, filled with a grey charge; then carry a leader from the tail of one cafe to the mouth of the other.

Globes for thefe wheels are made of 2 tin hoops, with their edges outwards, fixed one within the other, at right angles. The diameter of thefe hoops muft be fomewhat lefs than that of the wheel. Having made a globe, drive in the centre of a wheel an iron fpindle, which muft ftand perpendicular, and its length 4 or 6 inches more than the diameter of the globe.

This fpindle ferves for an axis, on which the globe is fixed, which, when done, muft ftand 4 or 6 inches from the wheel: round one fide of each hoop muft be foldered little bits of tin, 2 $\frac{1}{2}$ inches diftance from each other; which pieces muft be 2 inches in length each, and only faftened at one end, the other ends being left loofe, to turn round the fmall port fires, and hold them on: thefe port fires muft be made of fuch a length, as will laft out the cafes on the wheel. You are to obferve, that there need not be any port fires at the bottom of the globe within 4 inches of the fpindle; for, if there were, they would have no effect, but only burn the wheel: all the port fires muft be placed perpendicular from the centre of the globe, with their mouths outwards; and muft all be clothed with leaders, fo as all to take fire with the fecond cafe of the wheel; which cafes muft burn 2 at a time, 1 oppofite the other. When 2 cafes of a wheel begin together, 2 will end together; therefore the 2 oppofite end cafes muft have their ends pinched and fecured from fire. The method of firing fuch wheels is, by carrying a leader from the mouth of one of the firft cafes, to that of the other, which leader being burnt through the middle, will give fire to both at the fame time.

Odoriferous Water Balloons.

Thefe balloons are made in the fame manner, as air balloons, but very thin of paper, and in diameter 1 $\frac{1}{4}$ inch with a vent of $\frac{1}{2}$ an inch diameter. The fhells being
made,

made, and quite dry, fill them with any of the following compositions, which must be rammed in tight: these balloons must be fired at the vent, and put into a bowl of water. Odoriferous works are generally fired in rooms.

Composition I.

Saltpetre 2 oz. flower of sulphur 1 oz. camphor ½ oz. yellow amber ½ oz. charcoal dust ½ oz. flower of benjamin, or assa odorata, ¼ oz. all powdered very fine, and well mixed.

Composition II.

Saltpetre 12 oz. meal powder 3 oz. frankincense 1 oz. myrrh ½ oz. camphor ½ oz. charcoal 3 oz. all moistened with the oil of spike.

Composition III.

Saltpetre 2 oz. sulphur ½ oz. antimony ½ oz. amber ½ oz. cedar raspings ¼ oz. all mixed with the oil of roses, and a few drops of bergamot.

Composition IV.

Saltpetre 4 oz. sulphur 1 oz. saw-dust of juniper ¼ oz. saw-dust of cypress 1 oz. camphor ¼ oz. myrrh 2 drams, dried rosemary ¼ oz. cortex elaterii ¼ oz. all moistened a little with the oil of roses.

N. B. Water rockets may be made with any of the above compositions, with a little alteration, to make them weaker or stronger, according to the size of the cases.

Water Balloons.

Having made some thin paper shells, of what diameter you please, fill some with the composition for water balloons, and some after this manner. Having made

the

the vent of the shels pretty large, fill them almoft full with water rockets, marrons, fquibs, &c. Then put in fome blowing powder, fufficient to burft the fhells, and afterwards fix in the vent a water rocket, long enou h to reach the bottom of the fhell, and its neck to project a little out of the vent; this rocket muft be open at the end, to fire the powder in the fhell, which will burft the fhell, and difperfe the fmall rockets, &c. in the water. When you have well fecured the large rocket in the vent of the fhell, take a cork float with a hole in its middle, which fit over the head of the rocket, and faften it to the fhell: this float muft be large enough to keep the balloon above water.

Water Squibs

Are generally made of 1 oz. ferpent cafes, 7 or 8 inches long, filled 2 3ds with charge, and the remainder bounced. The common method of firing them is, — Take a water wheel, with a tin mortar in its centre, which load with fquibs, after the ufual method; but the powder in the mortar muft be no more than will juft throw the fquibs out (eafily into the water): you may place the cafes on the wheel, either obliquely, or horizontally; and on the top of the wheel, round the mortar, fix fix cafes of brilliant fire, perpendicular to the wheel: thefe cafes muft be fired at the beginning of the laft cafe of the wheel, and the mortar, at the conclufion of the fame.

A Sea Fight with fmall Ships, and to prepare a Fire-fhip for it.

Having procured 4 or 5 fmall fhips, of 2 or 3 feet in length, (or as many as you defign to fight) make a number of fmall reports, which are to ferve for guns. Of thefe range as many as you pleafe, on each fide of the upper decks; then at the head and ftern of each fhip fix a 2 oz. cafe, 8 inches long, filled with a flow port-fire receipt; but take care to place it in fuch a manner,

that

that the fire may fall in the water, and not burn the rigging: in these cafes bore holes at unequal diftances from one another, but make as many in each cafe, as half the number of reports, fo that one cafe may fire the guns on one fide, and the other thofe on the oppofite. The method of firing the guns, is, by carrying a leader, from the holes in the cafes, to the reports on the decks; you muft make thefe leaders very fmall, and be careful in calculating the burning of the flow fire, in the regulating cafes, that more than 2 guns be not fired at a time. When you would have a broadfide given, let a leader be carried to a cracker, placed on the outfide of the fhip, which cracker muft be tied loofe, or the reports will be too flow; in all the fhips put artificial guns at the port holes.

Having filled, and bored holes, in two port fires, for regulating the guns in one fhip, make all the reft exactly the fame; then when you begin the engagement, light one fhip firft, and fet it a failing, and fo on with the reft, fending them out fingly, which will make them fire regularly, at different times, without confufion; for the time between the firing of each gun will be equal to that of lighting the flow fires.

The fire fhip may be of any fize, and need not be very good, for it is always loft in the action. To prepare a fhip for this purpofe, make a port fire equal in fize with them in the other fhips, and place it at the ftern; in every port place a large port fire, filled with a very ftrong compofition, and painted in imitation of a gun, and let them all be fired at once by a leader from the flow fire, within 2 or 3 diameters of its bottom; all along both fides, on the top of the upper deck, lay ftar compofition about ½ an inch thick, and 1 broad, which muft be wetted with thin fize, then primed with meal powder, and fecured from fire by pafting paper over it; in the place where you lay this compofition, drive fome little tacks with flat heads, to hold it faft to the deck: this muft be fired juft after the fham guns, and when burning will fhew a flame all round the fhip: at the head take up the decks, and put in a tin mortar loaded

with

with crackers, which mortar muſt be fired by a pipe
from the end of the ſlow fire; the firing of this mortar
will ſink the ſhip, and make a pretty concluſion. The
regulating port fire of this ſhip muſt be lighted at the
ſame time with the firſt fighting ſhip.

Having prepared all the ſhips for fighting, we ſhall
next proceed with the management of them, when on
the water. At one end of the pond, juſt under the ſur-
face of the water, fix 2 running blocks, at what diſtance
you chuſe the ſhips ſhould fight; and at the other end
of the pond, oppoſite to each of theſe blocks, under the
water, fix a double block; then on the land, by each of
the double blocks, place two ſmall windlaſſes; round
one of them turn one end of a ſmall cord, and the other
end put through one of the blocks; then carry it through
the ſingle one, at the oppoſite end of the pond, and
bring it back through the double block again, and
round the other windlaſs: to this cord, near the double
block, tie as many ſmall ſtrings, as half the number of
the ſhips, at what diſtance you think proper; but theſe
ſtrings muſt not be more than 2 feet each: the looſe end
of each make faſt to a ſhip, juſt under her bow-ſprit;
but if tied to the keel, or too near the water, it will
overſet the ſhip. Half the ſhips being thus prepared,
near the other double block fix two more windlaſſes,
to which faſten a cord, and to it tie the other half of the
ſhips, as before: when you fire the ſhips, pull in the
cord, with one of the windlaſſes, to get all the ſhips together; and when you have ſet fire to the firſt, turn
that windlaſs, which draws them out, and ſo on with
the reſt, till they are all out, in the middle of the pond;
then by turning the other windlaſs, you will draw them
back again; by which method you may make them
change ſides, and tack about, backwards and forwards,
at pleaſure. For the fire-ſhip, fix the blocks and windlaſſes between the others, ſo that when ſhe ſails out, ſhe
will be between the other ſhips: you muſt not let this
ſhip advance, till the guns at her ports take fire.

To fire Sky Rockets under Water,

You must have stands made as usual, only the rails must be placed flat, instead of edgeways, and have holes in them for the rocket sticks to go through; for if they were hung upon hooks, the motion of the water would throw them off: the stands being made, if the pond is deep enough, sink them at the sides, so deep, that when the rockets are in, their heads may just appear above the surface of the water; to the mouth of each rocket fix a leader, which put through the hole with the stick; then a little above the water must be a board, supported by the stand, and placed along a side of the rockets; then the ends of the leaders are turned up through holes made in this board, exactly opposite the rockets. By this means you may fire them singly, or all at once. Rockets may be fired by this method, in the middle of a pond, by a Neptune, a swan, a water wheel, or any thing else you chuse.

To represent Neptune in his Chariot.

To do this to perfection, you must have a Neptune made (of wood, or basket work) as big as life, fixed on a float, large enough to bear his weight; on which must be 2 horses heads, and necks, so as to seem swimming, as shown by Fig. 35. For the wheels of the chariot, there must be 2 vertical wheels of black fire, and on Neptune's head a horizontal wheel, of brilliant fire, with all its cases, to play upwards. When this wheel is made, cover it with paper, or pasteboard, cut and painted like Neptune's coronet; then let the trident be made without prongs, but instead of them, fix 3 cases of a weak grey charge, and on each horse's head put an 8 oz. case of brilliant fire, and on the mouth of each fix a short case, of the same diameter, filled with the white flame receipt, enough to last out all the cases on the wheels: these short cases must be open at bottom, that they may light the brilliant fires; for the horses eyes put small port fires, and in

each

each noſtril put a ſmall caſe filled half with grey charge, and the reſt with port-fire compoſition.

If Neptune is to give fire to any building on the water; at his firſt ſetting out, the wheels of the chariot, and that on his head, with the white flames on the horſes heads, and the port fires in their eyes and noſtrils, muſt all be lighted at once; then from the bottom of the white flames carry a leader to the trident. As Neptune is to advance by the help of a block and cord, you muſt manage it ſo as not to let him turn about, till the brilliant fires on the horſes, and the trident, begin; for it is by the fire from the horſes, (which plays almoſt upright) that the building, or work, is lighted; which muſt be thus prepared. From the mouth of the caſe, which is to be firſt fired, hang ſome looſe quick-match, to receive the fire from the horſes. When Neptune is only to be ſhewn by himſelf, without ſetting fire to any other works; let the white flames on the horſes be very ſhort, and not to laſt longer than one caſe of each wheel, and let 2 caſes of each wheel burn at a time.

Swans and Ducks in Water.

If you would have the ſwans, or ducks, diſcharge rockets into the water, they muſt be made hollow, and of paper, and filled with ſmall water rockets, with ſome blowing powder, to throw them out; but if this is not done, they may be made of wood, which will laſt many times. Having made and painted ſome ſwans, fix them on floats; then in the places where their eyes ſhould be, bore holes two inches deep, inclining downwards, and wide enough to receive a ſmall port fire; the port fire caſes for this purpoſe muſt be made of braſs, 2 inches long, and filled with a ſlow bright charge; in the middle of one of theſe caſes make a little hole, then put the port fire in the eye hole of the ſwan, leaving about half an inch to project out, and in the other eye put another port fire, with a hole made in it; then in the neck of the ſwan, within two inches of one of the eyes,

bore

bore a hole flantways, to meet that in the port fire; in this hole put a leader, and carry it to a water rocket, that muft be fixed under the tail with its mouth upwards; on the top of the head place 2 one-ounce cafes, 4 inches long each, drove with brilliant fire; one of thefe cafes muft incline forwards, and the other backwards; thefe muft be lighted at the fame time as the water rocket; to do which, bore a hole between them, in the top of the fwan's head, down to the hole in the port fire, to which carry a leader; if the fwan is filled with rockets, they muft be fired by a pipe, from the end of the water rocket under the tail. When you fet the fwan a fwimming, light the 2 eyes.

Water Fire-Fountains.

. To make a fire fountain, you muft firft have a float made of wood, 3 feet diameter, then in the middle fix a round perpendicular poft, 4 feet high, and 2 inches diameter; round this poft fix 3 circular wheels, made of thin wood, without any fpokes. The largeft of thefe wheels muft be placed within 2 or 3 inches of the float, and muft be nearly of the fame diameter. The 2d wheel muft be 2 feet 2 inches diameter, and fixed at 2 feet diftance from the firft. The 3d wheel muft be 1 foot 4 inches diameter, and fixed within 6 inches of the top of the poft: the wheels being fixed, take 18 four or 8 ounce cafes, of brilliant fire, and place them round the firft wheel, with their mouths outwards, and inclining downwards; on the 2d wheel place 13 cafes of the fame, and in the fame manner, as thofe on the firft; on the 3d place 8 more of thefe cafes, in the fame manner as before, and on the top of the poft fix a gerbe; then clothe all the cafes with leaders, fo that both they and the gerbe may take fire at the fame time. Before you fire this work, try it in the water, to fee if the float is properly made, fo as to keep the fountain upright.

SECT.

SECT. VI.—Crackers.

CUT some cartridge paper into pieces 3 ½ inches bread, and 1 foot long; 1 edge of each fold down lengthwise about ¼ of an inch broad; then fold the double edge down ¼ of an inch, and turn the single edge back half over the double fold; then open it, and lay all along the channel, which is formed by the folding of the paper, some meal powder; then fold it over and over, till all the paper is doubled up, rubbing it down every turn; this done, bend it backwards and forwards, 2 ½ inches, or thereabouts, at a time, as oft as the paper will allow; then hold all these folds flat and close, and with a small pinching cord give one turn round the middle of the cracker, and pinch it close; then bind it with pack-thread, as tight as you can; then in the place where it was pinched, prime one end of it, and cap it with touch-paper. When these crackers are fired, they will give a report at every turn of the paper: if you would have a great number of bounces, you must cut the paper longer, or join them after they are made; but if they are made very long before they are pinched, you must have a piece of wood with a groove in it, deep enough to let in half the cracker: this will hold it straight, while it is pinching. Fig. 36. represents a cracker complete.

Single Reports.

Cases for reports are generally rolled on 1 and 2 oz. formers, and seldom made larger, but on particular occasions; they are made from 2 to 4 inches long, and very thick of paper: having rolled a case, pinch one end quite close, and drive it down; then fill the case with corn powder, only leaving room to pinch it at top; but before you pinch it, put in a piece of paper at top of the powder.

powder. Reports are fired by a vent, bored in the middle, or at one end, just as required.

Marrons.

Formers for marrons are from ¾ of an inch, to 1½ diameter. Cut the paper for the cases twice the diameter of the former broad, and long enough to go 3 times round; when you have rolled a case, paste down the edge, and tie one end close; then with the former drive it down to take away the wrinkles, and make it flat at bottom; then fill the case with corn powder 1 diameter and ¼ high, and fold down the rest of the case tight on the powder. The marron being thus made, wax some strong pack-thread with shoemakers wax; this thread wind up in a ball, then unwind 2 or 3 yards of it, and that part which is near the ball, make fast to a hook; then take a marron, and stand as far from the hook as the pack-thread will reach, and wind it lengthwise round the marron as close as you can, till it will hold no more that way; then turn it and wind the pack-thread on the short way, then lengthwise again, and so on till the paper is all covered; then make fast the end of the pack-thread, and beat down both ends of the marron, to bring it in shape. The method of firing marrons, is by making a hole at one end with an awl, and putting in a piece of quick-match; then take a piece of strong paper, in which wrap up the marron, with 2 leaders, which must be put down to the vent, and the paper tied tight round them with small twine; these leaders are bent on each side, and their loose ends tied to other marrons, and are nailed in the middle to the rail of the stand, as in Fig. 37. The use of winding the pack-thread in a ball is, that you may let it out as you want it, according to the quantity the marron may require; and that it may not be tied in knots, which would spoil the marron.

Marron

Marron Batteries,

If well managed, will keep time to a march, or a flow
piece of mufic. Marron batteries are made of feveral
ftands, with a number of crofs rails, for the marrons,
which are regulated by leaders, by cutting them of different lengths, and nailing them tight, or loofe, according to the time of the mufic. In marron batteries you
muft ufe the large and fmall marrons, and the nails for
the pipes muft have flat heads.

Line Rockets

Are made and drove as the fky rockets, but have no
heads; and the cafes muft be cut clofe to the clay; they
are fometimes made with 6 or 7 changes, but in general
not more than 4 or 5: the method of managing thofe
rockets is,—Firft, have a piece of light wood, the length
of 1 of the rockets, turned round about 2 $\frac{1}{4}$ inches diameter, with a hole through the middle lengthwife, large
enough for the line to go eafily through: if you defign
4 changes, have 4 grooves cut in the fwivel, one oppofite
the other, to lay the rockets in.

The mouths of the rockets being rubbed with wet
meal powder, lay them in the grooves, head to tail,
and tie them faft; from the tail of the firft rocket carry
a leader to the mouth of the fecond, and from the fecond
to the third, and fo on to as many as there are on the
fwivel, making every leader very fecure; but in fixing
thefe pipes, take care that the quick-match does not
enter the bores of the rockets: the rockets being fixed
on the fwivel, and ready to be fired, have a line 100 yards
long, ftretched and fixed up tight, at any height from
the ground; but be fure to place it horizontal: this length
of line will do for $\frac{1}{4}$ lb. rockets; but, if larger, the line
muft be longer: before you put up the line, put one
end of it through the fwivel, and when you fire the line
rocket, let the mouth of that rocket which you fire firft,
face that end of the line where you ftand; then the firft

rocket

rocket will carry the reft to the other end of the line, and the fecond will bring them back, and fo they will run out and in according to the number of rockets : at each end of the line, there muft be a piece of flat wood, for the rocket to ftrike againft, or its force will cut the line. Let the line be well foaped, and the hole in the fwivel very fmooth.

Different Decorations for Line Rockets.

To line rockets may be fixed great variety, fuch as flying dragons, mercuries, fhips, &c. Or they may be made to run on the line like a wheel, which is done in this manner. Have a flat fwivel, made very exact, and on it tie two rockets obliquely, one on each fide, which will make it turn round all the way it goes, and form a circle of fire ; the charge for thefe rockets fhould be a little weaker than common; if you would fhew 2 dragons fighting, get 2 fwivels made fquare, and on each tie 3 rockets together, on the under fide ; then have 2 flying dragons made of tin, and fix one of them on the top of each fwivel, fo as to ftand upright ; in the mouth of each dragon put a fmall cafe of common fire, and another at the end of the tail ; you may put 2 or 3 port fires, of a ftrong charge, on 1 fide of their bodies, to fhew them. This done, put them on the line, one at each end ; but let there be a fwivel in the middle of the line, to keep the dragons from ftriking together : before you fire the rockets light the cafes on the dragons, and if care be taken in firing both at the fame time, they will meet in the middle of the line, and feem to fight. Then they will run back, and return with great violence; which will have a very pleafing effect. The line for thefe rockets muft be very long, or they will ftrike too hard together.

Chinefe Flyers.

Cafes for flyers may be made of different fizes, from 1 to 8 ounces: they muft be made thick of paper, and 8 interior diameters long; they are rolled in the fame

H   manner

manner as tourbillons, with a ſtraight paſted edge, and pinched cloſe at one end. The method of filling them is, the caſe being put in a mould, whoſe cylinder, or foot, muſt be flat at top without a nipple, fill it within ½ a diameter of the middle; then ram in ½ a diameter of clay, on that as much compoſition as before, on which drive ½ a diameter of clay; then pinch the caſe cloſe, and drive it down flat; after this is done, bore a hole exactly through the centre of the clay in the middle; then in the oppoſite ſides at both ends make a vent, and in that ſide you intend to fire firſt make a ſmall hole to the compoſition near the clay in the middle, from which carry a quick match, covered with a ſingle paper, to the vent at the other end; then when the charge is burnt on one ſide, it will, by means of the quick match, communicate to the charge in the other, (which may be of a different ſort). The flyers being thus made, put an iron pin, that muſt be fixed in the work on which they are to be fired, and on which they are to run: through the hole in the middle, on the end of this pin, muſt be a nut to keep the flyer from running off. If you would have them turn back again after they are burnt, make both the vents at the ends on the ſame ſide, which will alter its courſe the contrary way.

Table Rockets

Are deſigned merely to ſhew the truth of driving, and the judgement of a fire worker, they having no other effect, when fired, than ſpinning round, in the ſame place where they begin, till they are burnt out, and ſhewing nothing more than an horizontal circle of fire.

The method of making theſe rockets is— Have a cone turned out of hard wood, 2½ inches diameter, and as much high; round the baſe of it draw a line; on this line fix 4 ſpokes, 2 inches long each, ſo as to ſtand one oppoſite the other; then fill 4 nine-inch 1lb. caſes, with any ſtrong compoſition, within 2 inches of the top: theſe caſes are made like tourbillons, and muſt be rammed with the greateſt exactneſs.

Your rockets being filled, fix their open ends on the ſhort ſpokes; then in the ſide of each caſe bore a

hole

hole near the clay; all thefe holes, or vents, muft be
fo made that the fire of each cafe may act the fame way;
from thefe vents carry leaders to the top of the cone,
and tie them together. When you would fire the rockets,
fet them on a fmooth table, and light the leaders in the
middle, and all the cafes will fire together (fee Fig. 38.)
and fpin on the point of the cone.

Thefe rockets may be made to rife like tourbillons,
by making the cafes fhorter, and boring 4 holes in the
under fide of each at equal diftances: this being done,
they are called Double Tourbillons.

Note, all the vents in the under fide of the cafes muft
be lighted at once; and the fharp point of the cone cut
off, at which place make it fpherical.

To make Wheels and other Works incombuftible.

It being neceffary, when your works are new, to paint
them of fome dark colour; therefore, if inftead of which,
you make ufe of the following compofition, it will give
them a good colour, and in a great meafure prevent
their taking fire fo foon as if painted. Take brick duft,
coal afhes, and iron filings, of each an equal quantity,
and mix them with a double fize, made hot. With this
wafh over your works, and when dry wafh them over
again; this will preferve the wood greatly againft fire.
Let the brick-duft and afhes be beat to a fine powder.

Single Vertical Wheels.

There are different forts of vertical wheels, fome having their fells of a circular form, others of an hexagon,
octagon, or decagon form, or any number of fides, according to the length of the cafes you defign for the
wheel: your fpokes being fixed in the nave, nail flips
of tin, with their edges turned up, fo as to form grooves
for the cafes to lie in, from the end of one fpoke to another;
then tie your cafes in the grooves, head to tail, in the

H 2   fame

fame manner as thofe on the horizontal water wheel, fo that the cafes fucceffively taking fire from one another, will keep the wheel in an equal rotation. Two of thefe wheels are very oft fired together, one on each fide of a building, and both lighted at the fame time, and all the cafes filled alike, to make them keep time together, which they will do if made by the following directions. In all the cafes of both wheels, except the firft, on each wheel, drive 2 or 3 ladles full of flow fire, in any part of the cafes; but be careful to ram the fame quantity in each cafe, and in the end of one of the cafes, on each wheel, you may ram 1 ladle full of dead fire compofition, which muft be very lightly drove; you may alfo make many changes of fire, by this method.

Let the hole in the nave of the wheel be lined with brafs, and made to turn on a fmooth iron fpindle. On the end of this fpindle let there be a nut, to fcrew off and on; when you have put the wheel on the fpindle, fcrew on the nut, which will keep the wheel from flying off. Let the mouth of the firft cafe be a little raifed. See fig. 39. Vertical wheels are made from 10 inches to 3 feet diameter, and the fize of the cafes muft differ accordingly; 4 oz. cafes will do for wheels of 14 or 16 inches diameter, which is the proportion generally ufed. The beft wood for wheels of all forts, is a light and dry beech.

Horizontal Wheels

Are beft when their fells are made circular; in the middle of the top of the nave muft be a pintle, turned out of the fame piece as the nave, 2 inches long, and equal in diameter to the bore of 1 of the cafes of the wheel: there muft be a hole bored up the centre of the nave, within $\frac{1}{4}$ an inch of the top of the pintle. The wheel being made, nail at the end of each fpoke (of which there fhould be 6 or 8) a piece of wood, with a groove cut in it to receive the cafe. Thefe pieces fix in fuch a manner, that half the cafes may incline upwards, and

half

half downwards, and that when they are tied on, their heads and tails may come very near together: from the tail of one cafe to the mouth of the other carry a leader, which fecure with pafted paper. Befides thefe pipes, it will be neceffary to put a little meal powder infide the pafted paper, to blow off the pipe, that there may be no obftruction to the fire, from the cafes. By means of thefe pipes, the cafes will fucceffively take, burning one upwards, and the other downwards. On the pintle fix a cafe of the fame fort as thofe on the wheel; this cafe muft be fired by a leader, from the mouth of the laft cafe on the wheel, which cafe muft play downwards: inftead of a common cafe in the middle, you may put a cafe of Chinefe fire, long enough to burn as long as 2 or 3 of the cafes on the wheel.

Horizontal wheels are oft fired 2 at a time, and made to keep time, like vertical wheels; only they are made without any flow or dead fire; 10 or 12 inches will be enough for the diameter of wheels with 6 fpokes. Fig. 40. reprefents a wheel on fire, with the firft cafe burning.

Spirali Wheels

Are only double horizontal wheels, and made thus: The nave muft be about 6 inches long, and fomewhat thicker than the fingle fort; inftead of the pintle at top, make a hole for the cafe to be fixed in; and 2 fets of fpokes, one fet near the top of the nave, and the other near the bottom. At the end of each fpoke cut a groove, wherein you tie the cafes, there being no fell; the fpokes fhould not be more than $3\frac{1}{4}$ inches long each from the nave, fo that the wheel may not be more than 8 or 9 inches diameter; the cafes are placed in fuch a manner, that thofe at top play down, and thofe at bottom play up, but let the 2d or 4th cafe play horizontally. The cafe in the middle may begin with any of the others, you pleafe: 6 fpokes will be enough for each fet, fo that the wheel may confift of 12 cafes, befides that on the top: the cafes 6 inches each.

H 3

Plural

Plural Wheels

Are made to turn horizontally, and to confift of 3 fets
of fpokes, placed 6 at top, 6 at bottom, and 4 in the middle, which muft be a little fhorter than the reft: let the
diameter of the wheel be 10 inches; the cafes muft be
tied on the ends of the fpokes, in grooves cut on purpofe,
or in pieces of wood nailed on the ends of the fpokes,
with grooves cut in them as ufual: in clothing thefe
wheels, make the upper fet of cafes play obliquely
downwards, and them at bottom obliquely upwards,
and them in the middle horizontally. In placing the
leaders, you muft order it fo that the cafes may burn
thus, viz. firft up, then down, then horizontal, and fo
on with the reft; but another change may be made, by
driving in the end of the eighth cafe, 2 or 3 ladles full
of flow fire, to burn till the wheel has ftopped its courfe;
then let the other cafes be fixed the contrary way, which
will make the wheel run back again: for the cafe at
top you may put a fmall gerbe; and let the cafes on the
fpokes be fhort, and filled with a ftrong brilliant charge.

Illuminated Spiral Wheel.

Firft have a circular horizontal wheel, made 2 feet
diameter, with a hole quite through the nave; then take
3 thin pieces of deal, 3 feet long each, and ¾ of an inch
broad each: one end of each of thefe pieces nail to the fell
of the wheel, at an equal diftance from one another, and
the other end nail to a block with a hole in its bottom,
which muft be perpendicular with that in the block of the
wheel, but not fo large. The wheel being thus made,
have a hoop planed down very thin and flat; then nail one
end of it to the fell of the wheel, and wind it round the
3 fticks in a fpiral line, from the wheel to the block at top:
on the top of this block fix a cafe of Chinefe fire; on the
wheel you may place any number of cafes, which muft
incline downwards, and burn 2 at a time. If the wheel
fhould confift of 10 cafes, you may let the illuminations
and

and Chinefe fire begin with the fecond cafes. The fpindle for this wheel muft be a little longer than the cone, and made very fmooth at top, on which the upper block is to turn, and the whole weight of the wheel to reft. See Fig. 41.

Double Spiral Wheel.

For this wheel the block, or nave, muft be as long as the height of the worms, or fpiral lines, but muft be made very thin, and as light as poffible. In this block muft be fixed feveral fpokes, which muft diminifh, in length, from the wheel to the top, fo as not to exceed the furface of a cone of the fame height. To the ends of thefe fpokes nail the worms, which muft crofs each other feveral times: thefe worms clothe with illumina-, tions, the fame as thofe on the fingle wheels; but the horizontal wheel you may clothe as you like. At top of the worm place a cafe of fpur-fire, or an amber light. See Fig. 42. This figure is fhewn without leaders, to prevent a confufion of lines.

Ballóon Wheels

Are made to turn horizontally: they muft be made 2 feet diameter, without any fpokes, and very ftrong, with any number of fides. On the top of a wheel range and fix tin pots, 3 inches diameter, and 7 inches high each, as many of thefe as there are cafes on the wheel: near the bottom of each pot make a fmall vent; into each of thefe vents carry a leader from the tail of each cafe; fome of the pots load with ftars, and fome with ferpents, crackers, &c. As the wheels turn, the pots will fuc-ceffively be fired, and throw into the air a great variety of fires.

Fruiloni Wheels.

Firft have a nave made 9 inches long, and 3 in diame-ter: near the bottom of this nave fix 8 fpokes, with a hole

hole in the end of each, large enough to receive a 2 or 4 ounce cafe: each of thefe fpokes may be 14 inches long from the block. Near the top of this block fix 8 more of the fame fpokes, exactly over the others, but not fo long by 2 inches. As this wheel is to run horizontally, all the cafes in the fpokes at top muft play obliquely upwards, and all them in the fpokes at bottom obliquely downwards. This being done, have a fmall horizontal wheel made with 8 fpokes, each 5 inches long from the block: on the top of this wheel place a cafe of brilliant fire: all the cafes on this wheel muft play in an oblique direction downwards, and burn 2 at a time, and thofe on the large wheel 4 at a time; that is, 2 of thofe in the top fet of fpokes, and 2 of them in the bottom fet of fpokes.

The 4 firft cafes on the large wheel, and the 2 firft on the fmall, muft be fired at the fame time, and the brilliant fire at top, at the beginning of the laft cafes. The cafes of the wheels may be filled with a grey charge. When thefe wheels are completed, you muft have a ftrong iron fpindle, made 4 feet 6 long, and fixed perpendicular on the top of a ftand: on this put the large wheel, whofe nave muft have a hole quite through from the bottom to the top. This hole muft be large enough to turn eafy round the bottom of the fpindle, at which place there muft be a fhoulder, to keep the wheel from touching the ftand: at the top of the fpindle put the fmall wheel, and join it to a large one with a leader, in order to fire them both together.

Port-Fires for Illuminations

Have their cafes made very thin of paper, and rolled on formers, from 2 to 5 8ths of an inch diameter, and are made from 2 to 6 inches long: they are pinched clofe at one end, and left open at the other: when you fill them, put in but a little compofition at a time, and ram it in lightly, fo as not to break the cafe: 3 or 4 rounds of paper, with the laft round pafted, will be ftrong enough for thefe cafes.   Common

Common Port-Fires

Are intended purpofely to fire the works, their fire being very flow, and the heat of the flame fo intenfe, that, if applied to rockets, leaders, &c. it will fire them immediately. Port fires may be made of any length, but are feldom made more than 21 inches long: the interior diameter of port-fire moulds fhould be 10 16ths of an inch, and the diameter of the former, ½ an inch. The cafes muft be rolled wet with pafte, and one end pinched, or folded down. The moulds fhould be made of brafs, and to take in 2 pieces lengthwife; then, when the cafe is in the 2 fides, they are held together by brafs rings, or hoops, which are made to fit over the outfide. The bore of the mould muft not be made quite through, fo that there will be no occafion for a foot. Thofe port fires, when ufed, are held in copper fockets, fixed on the end of a long ftick: thefe fockets are made like port crayons, only with a fcrew, inftead of a ring.

Cafcades of Fire

Are made of any fize; but one made according to the dimenfions of that fhewn in Plate 4. Fig. 43. will be large enough for 8 oz cafes. Let the diftance from A to B, be 3 feet; from B to C, 2 feet 6 inches; and from C D, 2 feet; and let the crofs piece at A, be 4 feet long; then from each end of this piece, draw a line to D; then make the other crofs pieces fo long as to come within thofe lines. The top piece D, may be of any length fo as to hold the cafes, at a little diftance from each other; all the crofs pieces are fixed horizontally, and fupported by brackets; the bottom crofs piece fhould be about 1 foot 6 inches broad in the middle, the fecond 1 foot, the third 9 inches, and the top piece 4 inches: the cafes may be made of any length, but muft be filled with a brilliant charge. On the edges of the crofs pieces muft be nailed bits of wood, with a groove cut in each piece, large

enough

enough for a cafe to lie in. Thefe bits of wood are fixed fo as to incline downwards, and that the fire from one tier of cafes may play over the other. All the cafes being tied faft on, carry leaders from one to the other, and let there be a pipe hang from the mouth of one of the cafes, covered at the end with a fingle paper, which you burn to fire the cafcade.

The Fire-Tree.

To make a fire-tree, as fhewn by Fig. 44. you muft firft have a piece of wood 6 feet long, and 3 inches fquare; then at E, 9 inches from the top, make a hole in the front, and in each fide; or, inftead of holes, you may fix fhort pegs, to fit the infide of the cafes. At F, 9 inches from E, fix 3 more pegs; at G, 1 foot 9 inches from F, fix 3 pegs; at H, 9 inches from G, fix 3 pegs; at I, 9 inches from H, fix 3 pegs, inclining downwards; but all the other pegs muft incline upwards, that the cafes may have the fame inclination as you fee in the figure: then at top place a 4-inch mortar, loaded with ftars, rains, or crackers. In the middle of this mortar place a cafe filled with any fort of charge, but let it be fired with the other cafes: a brilliant charge will do for all the cafes; but the mortar may be made of any diameter, and the tree of any fize; and on it any number of cafes, provided they are placed in the manner defcribed.

Chinefe Fountains.

To make a Chinefe fountain, you muft have a perpendicular piece of wood, 7 feet long, and 2¼ inches fquare. 16 inches from the top, fix on the front a crofs piece 1 inch thick, and 2¼ broad, with the broad fide up: below this, fix 3 more pieces, of the fame width and thicknefs, at 16 inches from each other: let the bottom rail be 5 feet long, and the others of fuch a length as to allow the fire pumps to ftand in the middle of the intervals of each other. The pyramid being thus made, fix in the holes made in the bottom rail, 5 fire pumps, at

equal

equal diftances; on the 2d rail place 4 pumps; on the
3 d, 3; on the 4th, 2; and on the top of the poft, 1: but
place them all to incline a little forwards, that, when
they throw out the ftars, they may not ftrike againft the
crofs rails. Having fixed your fire pumps, clothe them
with leaders, fo that they may all be fired together.
See Fig. 45.

Of Illuminated Globes with Horizontal
Wheels.

The hoops for thefe globes may be made of wood,
tin, or iron wire, about 2 feet diameter. For a fingle
globe take 2 hoops, and tie them together, one within
the other, at right angles; then have a horizontal wheel
made, whofe diameter muft be a little wider than the
globe, and its nave 6 inches long, on the top of which
the globe is fixed, fo as to ftand 3 or 4 inches from
the wheel: on this wheel you may put any number of
cafes, filled with what charge you like; but let 2 of them
burn at a time: they may be placed horizontally, or to
incline downwards, juft as you chufe. Now, when the
wheel is clothed, fix on the hoops as many illuminations
as will ftand within 2 ½ inches of each other: thefe you
faften on the hoops with fmall iron binding-wire; and
when they are all on, put on your pipes of communication, which muft be fo managed, as to light them all with
the 2d or 3d cafe on the wheel. The fpindle on which
the globe is to run muft go through the block of the
wheel, up to the infide of the top of the globe, where
muft be fixed a bit of brafs, or iron, with a hole in
it to receive the point of the fpindle, on which the
whole weight of the wheel is to bear, as in Fig. 46,
which reprefents a globe on its fpindle. By this method
may be made a crown, which is done by having the
hoops bent in the form of a crown. Sometimes globes
and crowns are ordered fo as to ftand ftill, and the
wheel only to turn round; but when you would
have the globe or crown to ftand ftill, and the wheel

to run by itself, the block of the wheel must not be so long, nor the spindle any longer than to just raise the globe a little above the wheel; and the wheel cases and illumination must begin together.

Dodecaedron.

So called because it nearly represents a twelve-sided figure, and is made thus. First have a ball turned out of some hard wood, 14 inches diameter: when done, divide its surface into 14 equal parts, from which bore holes 1 ½ inch diameter, perpendicular to the centre, so that they may all meet in the middle: then let there be turned in the inside of each hole a female screw; and to all the holes, but one, must be made a round spoke 5 feet long, with 4 inches of the screw at one end, to fit the holes; then in the screw end of all the spokes bore a hole, 5 inches up, which must be bored slanting, so as to come out at one side, a little above the screw; from which cut a small groove along the spoke, within 6 inches of the other end, where you make another hole through to the other side of the spoke: in this end fix a spindle, on which put a small wheel, of 3 or 4 sides, each side 6 or 7 inches long: these sides must have grooves cut in them, large enough to receive a 2 or 4 oz. case: when these wheels are clothed, put them on the spindles, and at the end of each spindle put a nut to keep the wheel from falling off: the wheels being thus fixed, carry a pipe from the mouth of the first case on each wheel, thro' the hole in the side of the spoke, and from thence along the groove, and through the other hole, so as to hang out at the screw end about an inch. The spokes being all prepared in this manner, you must have a post, on which you intend to fire the work, with an iron screw in the top of it, to fit one of the holes in the ball: on this screw fix the ball; then in the top hole of the ball put a little meal powder, and some loose quick-match; then screw in all the spokes, and in one side of the ball bore a hole, in which put a leader, and secure it at the end; and your work will be ready to be fired. By this leader the powder

der and match in the centre is fired, which will light the match at the ends of the spokes all at once, whereby all the wheels will be lighted at once. There may be an addition to this piece, by fixing a small globe on each wheel, or 1 on the top wheel only. A grey charge will be proper for the wheel cases.

The Yew Tree of Brilliant Fire

Is reprefented by Fig. 47. as it appears when burning. First, let A be an upright piece of wood, 4 feet long, 2 inches broad, and 1 thick: at top of this piece, on the flat fide, fix a hoop, 14 inches diameter; and round its edge and front place illuminations; and in the centre a 5-pointed star; then at E, which is $1\frac{1}{4}$ foot from the edge of the hoop, place 2 cafes of brilliant fire, 1 on each fide: thefe cafes fhould be 1 foot long each: below thefe fix 2 more cafes of the fame fize, and at fuch a diftance, that their mouths may almoft meet them at top: then, clofe to the ends of thefe cafes, fix 2 more of the fame cafes; they muft ftand parallel to them at E. The cafes being thus fixed, clothe them with leaders; fo that they, with the illuminations and ftar at top, may all take fire together.

Stars with Points for Regulated Pieces, &c.

Thefe ftars are made of different fizes, according to the work for which they are intended: they are made with cafes from 1 oz. to 1 lb. but in general with 4 oz. cafes, 4 or 5 inches long: the cafes muft be rolled with pafte, and twice as thick of paper as a rocket of the fame bore. Having rolled a cafe, pinch one end of it quite clofe; then drive in $\frac{1}{2}$ a diameter of clay, and when the cafe is dry, fill it with compofition, 2 or 3 inches, to the length of the cafes, with which it is to burn: at top of the charge drive fome clay; as the ends of thefe cafes are feldom punched, they would be liable to take fire. Having filled a cafe, divide the circumference of it at the pinched end clofe to the clay into 5 equal parts; then

bore

bore 5 holes with a gimblet, about the size of the neck of a common 4 oz. case, into the composition: from one hole to the other carry a quick-match, and secure it with paper: this paper must be put on in the manner of that on the ends of wheel cases, so that the hollow part, which projects from the end of the case, may serve to receive a leader from any other work, to give fire to the points of the star. These stars may be made with any number of points.

Fixed Sun with a Transparent Face.

To make a sun of the best sort there should be 2 rows of cases, as in Fig. 48, which will shew a double glory, and make the rays strong and full. The frame, or sun wheel, must be made thus: Have a circular flat nave made very strong, 12 inches diameter: to this fix 6 strong flat spokes, A, B, C, D, E, F. On the front of these fix a circular fell, 5 feet diameter; within which fix another fell, the length of one of the sun cases less in diameter; within this fix a 3d fell, whose diameter must be less than the 2d, by the length of 1 case and 1 3d. The wheel being made, divide the fells into so many equal parts as you would have cases (which may be done from 24 to 44): at each division fix a flat iron staple: these staples must be made to fit the cases, to hold them fast on the wheel: let the staples be so placed, that one row of cases may lie in the middle of the intervals of the other.

In the centre of the block of the sun drive a spindle, on which put a small hexagon wheel, whose cases must be filled with the same charge as the cases of the sun: 2 cases of this wheel must burn at a time, and begin with them on the fells. Having fixed on all the cases, carry pipes of communication from one to the other, as you see in the figure, and from one side of the sun to the wheel in the middle, and from thence to the other side of the sun. These leaders will hold the wheel steady while the sun is fixing up, and will also

be

be a fure method of lighting both cafes of the wheel together.   A fun thus made is called a Brilliant fun, becaufe
the wood work is intirely covered with fire from the
wheel in the middle, fo that there appears nothing but
fparks of brilliant fire: but, if you would have a Tranfparent face in the centre, you muft have one made of
pafteboard, of any fize.   The method of making a face is,
by cutting out the eyes, nofe, and mouth, for the fparks of
the wheel to appear through; but, inftead of this face,
you may have one painted on oiled paper, or Perfian filk,
ftrained tight on a hoop; which hoop muft be fupported
by 3 or 4 pieces of wire at 6 inches diftance from the
wheel in the centre, fo that the light of it may illuminate
the face.   By this method you may have, in the front of
a fun, VIVAT REX, cut in pafteboard, or Apollo painted
on filk; but, for a fmall collection, a fun with a fingle
glory, and a wheel in front, will be moft fuitable.   ¼ lb.
cafes, filled 10 inches with compofition, will be a good
fize for a fun of 5 feet diameter; but, if larger, the cafes
muft be greater in proportion.

Three Vertical Wheels illuminated, which turn on their own Naves upon a Horizontal Table.

A plan of this is fhewn by Fig. 49.   Let D be a deal
table 3 feet (diameter: this table muft be fixed horizontally on the top of a poft; on this poft muft be a perpendicular iron fpindle, which muft come through the
centre of the table: then let A, B, C, be 3 fpokes joined
to a triangular flat piece of wood, in the middle of which
make a hole to fit eafily over the fpindle: let E, F, G,
be pieces of wood, 4 or 5 inches long each, and
2 inches fquare, fixed on the under fides of the fpokes;
in thefe pieces make holes lengthwife to receive the thin
part of the blocs of the wheels, which, when in, are
prevented from coming out by a fmall iron pin being run
through the end of each.   K, L, M, are 3 vertical octagon
wheels,

wheels, 18 inches diameter each: the blocks of thefe wheels muft be long enough for 3 or 4 inches to reft on the table ; round which part drive a number of fharp points of wire, which muft not project out of the blocks more than 1 16th of an inch: the ufe of thefe points is, that, when the blocks run round, they will ftick in the table, and help the wheels forward: if the naves are made of ftrong wood, one inch will be enough for the diameter of the thin part, which fhould be made to turn eafy in the holes in the pieces E, F, G. On the front of the wheels make 4 or 5 circles of ftrong wire, or flat hoops, and tie on them as many illuminations as they will hold at 2 inches from each other: inftead of circles, you may make fpiral lines, clothed with illuminations, at the fame diftance from each other as thofe on the hoops. When illuminations are fixed on a fpiral line in the front of a wheel, they muft be placed a little on the flant, the contrary way that the wheel runs: the cafes for thefe wheels may be filled with any coloured charge, but muft burn only one at a time.

The wheels being thus prepared, you muft have a globe, crown, or fpiral wheel, to put on the fpindle in the middle of the table: this fpindle fhould be juft long enough to raife the wheel of the globe, crown, or fpiral wheel, fo high that its fire may play over the 3 vertical wheels: by this means their fires will not be confufed, nor will the wheels receive any damage from the fire of each other. In clothing this work, let the leaders be fo managed, that all the wheels may light together, and the illuminations after 2 cafes of each wheel are burnt.

Illuminated Chandelier.

Illuminated works are much admired by the Italians, and indeed are a great addition to a collection of works: in a grand exhibition an illuminated piece fhould be fired after every 2 or 3 wheels, or fixed pieces of common and brilliant fires; and likewife illuminated works may be made cheap, quick, and eafy.

To

To make an illuminated chandelier, you muſt firſt have one made of thin wood.. See Fig. 50. The chandelier. being made, bore in the front of the branches, and in the body, and alſo in the crown at top, as many holes for illuminations· as they will contain, at 3 inches diſtance from each other: in theſe holes put illuminations filled with white, blue, or brilliant charge. Having fixed in the port fires, clothe them. with leaders, ſo that the chandelier and crown may light together. The ſmall circles on this figure repreſent the mouths of the illuminations, which muſt project ſtrait from the front.

Illuminated Yew-Tree.

Firſt have a tree made of wood, ſuch as is ſhewn by Fig. 51. The middle piece, or ſtem, on which the branches are fixed, muſt be 8 feet 6 inches high: at the bottom of this piece draw a line, at right angles, 2 feet 6 inches long at each ſide; then from L, which is 1 foot 6 inches from the bottom, draw a line on each ſide to C and D: theſe lines will give the length of the 2 firſt branches. Then put on the 2 top branches parallel to them at bottom: let the length of each of theſe branches be 1 foot from the ſtem: from the ends of theſe branches draw a line to C and D: then fix on 5 more branches at an = diſtance from each other, and their length will be determined by the lines A C and E D. When the branches are fixed, place illuminating port fires on the top of each, as many as you chuſe: behind the top of the ſtem faſten a gerbe, or white fountain, which muſt be fired at the beginning of the illuminations on the tree.

Flaming Stars with Brilliant Wheels.

To make a flaming ſtar, you muſt firſt have made a circular piece of ſtrong wood about 1 inch thick and 2 feet diameter: round this block fix 8 points, 2 feet 6 inches long each; 4 of theſe points muſt be ſtraight, and 4 flaming: theſe points being joined on very ſtrong, and even

I with

with the furface of the block, nail tin or pafteboard on their edges, from the block to the end of each, where they muft be joined: this tin muft project in front 8 inches, and be joined where they meet at the block; round the front of the block fix 4 pieces of thick iron wire, 8 inches long each, equally diftant from each other: this being done, cut a piece of pafteboard round, 2 feet diameter, and draw on it a ftar, as may be feen in Fig. 52. This ftar cut out, and on the back of it pafte oiled paper; then paint each point half red, and half yellow, lengthwife; but the body of the ftar muft be left open, wherein muft run a brilliant wheel, made thus: Have a light block turned 9 inches long; at each end of it fix 6 fpokes; at the end of each fpoke put a 2 oz. cafe of brilliant fire: the length of thefe cafes muft be in proportion to the wheel, and the diameter of the wheel when the cafes are on muft be a little lefs than the diameter of the body of the fmall ftar: the cafes on the fpokes in front muft have their mouths incline outwards, and them on the infide fpokes muft be placed fo as to form a vertical circle of fire. When you place your leaders, carry the firft pipe from the tail of 1 of the cafes in front to the mouth of 1 of the infide cafes, and from the tail of that to another in front, and fo on to all the cafes. Your wheel being made, put it on a fpindle, in the centre of the ftar; this fpindle muft have a fhoulder at bottom, to keep the wheel at a little diftance from the block. This wheel muft be kept on the fpindle by a nut at the end; having fixed on the wheel, faften the tranf-parent ftar to the 4 pieces of wire: when you fire it, you will only fee a common horizontal wheel; but when the firft cafe is burnt out, it will fire one of the vertical cafes, which will fhew the tranfparent ftar, and fill the large flames and points with fire; then it will again appear like a common wheel, and fo on for 12 changes.

Touch

Touch-Paper for Capping of Serpents, Crackers, &c.

Diffolve, in fpirits of wine or vinegar, a little faltpetre; then take fome purple or blue paper, and wet it with this liquor, and when dry it will be fit for ufe; when you pafte this paper on any of your works, take care that the pafte does not touch that part which is to burn. The method of ufing this paper is by cutting it into flips, long enough to go once round the mouth of a ferpent, tracker, &c. When you pafte on thefe flips, leave a little above the mouth of the cafe not pafted; then prime the cafe with meal powder, and twift the paper to a point.

Projected Regulated Piece of Nine Mutations.

A regulated piece, if well executed, is as curious a work as any in fireworks: it confifts of fixed and moveable pieces on one fpindle, reprefenting various figures, which take fire fucceffively one from another, without any affiftance after lighting the firft mutation; but, for the better explanation of this piece, I fhall give a full defcription of the method of communicating the fire from one mutation to the other, with a figure of each as they ftand on the fpindle. Regulated pieces are made of many kinds, and of any number of mutations, from 2 to 9, which is the greateft number I ever knew a piece to confift of, except one of my own making, which was compofed of 15 mutations, all different fires and figures: but, as an explanation of fo large a piece would be difficult to comprehend, I fhall omit it, leaving fo many changes to thofe who have made a great progrefs in this art, and only teach the manner of making a piece of 9 mutations, as fhewn in Plate V, Fig. 53. As it will be neceffary that every mutation fhould be feparately explained,

I 2   I fhall

I shall first give the name of each, with the colour of fire, and size of the case belonging to it; after which proceed with the proportion of each mutation, with the nature of the spindle, and placing the leaders.

First Mutation

Is a hexagon vertical wheel, illuminated in front with small port fires tied on the spokes; this wheel must be clothed with 2 oz. cases, filled with black charge; the length of these cases is determined by the size of the wheel, but must burn singly.

Second Mutation

Is a fixed piece, called a Golden Glory, by reason of the cases being filled with spur-fire; the cases must stand perpendicular to the block on which they are fixed, so that, when burning, they may represent a glory of fire: this mutation is generally composed of 5 or 7 2-oz. cases.

Third Mutation

Is moveable, and is only an octagon vertical wheel, clothed with 4 oz. cases, filled with brilliant charge; 2 of these cases must burn at a time: in this wheel you may make changes of fire.

Fourth Mutation

Is a fixed sun of brilliant fire, consisting of 12 4-oz. cases; the necks of these cases must be a little larger than those of 4 oz. wheel cases: in this mutation may be made a change of fire, by filling the cases half with brilliant charge, and half with grey.

Fifth Mutation

Is a fixed piece, called the Porcupine's Quills; this piece consists of 12 spokes, standing perpendicular to the

the block in which they are fixed; on each of thefe fpokes, near the end, muft be placed a 4 oz. cafe of brilliant fire; all thefe cafes muft incline either to the right or left, fo that they may all play one way.

Sixth Mutation

Is a ftanding piece, called the Crofs Fire. This mutation confifts of 8 fpokes fixed in a block; near the end of each of thofe fpokes muft be tied 2 4-oz. cafes of white charge, one acrofs the other, fo that the fires from the cafes on 1 fpoke may interfect the fire from cafes on the other.

Seventh Mutation

Is a fixed wheel, with 2 circular fells, on which are placed 16 8-ounce cafes of brilliant fire, in the form of a ftar; this piece is called a Fixed Star of Wild-fire.

Eighth Mutation.

This is a beautiful piece, called a Brilliant Star-piece: it confifts of 6 fpokes, which are ftrengthened by 2 fells of a hexagon form, at fome diftance from each other; at the end of each fpoke, in the front is fixed a brilliant ftar of 5 points; and on each fide of every ftar is placed a 4 oz. cafe of black or grey charge; thefe cafes muft be placed with their mouths fideways, fo that their fires may crofs each other.

Ninth Mutation

Is a wheel piece: this is compofed of 6 long fpokes, with a hexagon vertical wheel at the end of each; thefe wheels run on fpindles in the front of the fpokes; all the wheels are lighted together: 2 oz. cafes will do for thefe wheels, and may be filled with any coloured charge.

I 3

After

After having fpoke of the feveral parts of the regulated piece, each by their proper names and colour of fire, I fhall next proceed with the proportion of every mutation, with the method of conveying the fire from one to the other, and the diftance they ftand one from the other on the fpindle.

Firſt Mutation

Muſt be a hexagon vertical wheel, 14 inches diameter; on one fide of the block, whofe diameter is 2 ½ inches, is fixed a tin barrel, A, fee Fig. 53, No. 1, this barrel muſt be a little lefs in diameter than the nave; let the length of the barrel and block be 6 inches. Having fixed the cafes on the wheel, carry a leader from the tail of the laſt cafe into the tin barrel through a hole made on pur-pofe, 2 inches from the block; at the end of this leader let there be about 1 inch or 2 of loofe match; but take care to fecure well the hole wherein the pipe is put, to prevent any fparks falling in, which would light the fecond mutation before its time, and confufe the whole.

Second Mutation

Is thus made. Have a nave turned 2 ½ inches diame-ter, and 3 long; then let ¼ an inch of that end which faces the firſt wheel be turned fo as to fit eafy into the tin barrel of the firſt mutation, which muſt turn round it without touching; on the other end of the block fix a tin barrel, B, Nº. 2, this barrel muſt be 6 inches long, and only ½ an inch of it to fit on the block. Round the nave fix 5 fpokes, 1 ½ inch long each; the diameter of the fpokes muſt be equal to a 2 oz. former; on thefe fpokes put 5 7-inch 2-oz. cafes of fpur fire, and carry leaders from the mouth of one to the other, that they may all light together; then from the mouth of 1 of the cafes, carry a leader through a hole bored flantways in the nave, from between the fpokes, to the front of the block near the fpindle hole: the end of this leader muſt project out

of

of the hole into the barrel of the firſt mutation, ſo that when the pipe which comes from the end of the laſt caſe on the firſt wheel finiſhes, it may take fire, and light the 2d mutation. To communicate the fire to the 3d mutation, bore a hole near the bottom of one of the 5 caſes to the compoſition, and from thence carry a leader into a hole made in the middle of the barrel B; this hole muſt be covered with paſted paper.

Third Mutation

May be either an octagon or hexagon wheel, 20 inches diameter; let the nave be 3 ½ inches diameter, and 3 ½ in length; 1 ½ inch of the front of the nave muſt be made to fit in the barrel B. On the other end of the block fix a tin barrel, C, Nº. 3. this barrel muſt be 9 ½ inches in length, one inch of which muſt fit over the block. The caſes of this wheel muſt burn 2 at a time; and from the mouths of the 2 firſt caſes carry a leader, through holes in the nave, into the barrel of the ſecond mutation, after the uſual manner; but beſides theſe leaders let there be a pipe go acroſs the wheel from one firſt caſe to the other; then from the tail of one of the laſt caſes carry a pipe into a hole in the middle of the barrel C: at the end of this pipe let there hang ſome looſe quick match.

Fourth and Fifth Mutations.

I ſhall here ſpeak of thoſe 2 mutations under 1 head, as their naves are made of 1 piece, which from E to F is 14 inches; E, a block 4 inches diameter, with 10 or 12 ſhort ſpokes, on which are fixed 11 inch 8 oz. caſes: let the front of this block be made to fit eaſy in the barrel C, and clothe the caſes ſo that they may all light together; and let a pipe be carried through a hole in the block into the barrel C, in order to receive the fire from the leader brought from the laſt caſe on the wheel. G, the nave of the 5th mutation, whoſe diameter muſt be 4 ½ inches: in this nave fix 10 or 12 ſpokes 1 ½ foot in

I 4

length

length each; thefe fpokes muft ftand 7 inches diftant from the fpokes of the 4th mutation; and at the end of each fpoke tie a 4 oz. cafe, as N° 5. all thefe cafes are to be lighted together, by a leader brought from the end of 1 of the cafes on N°. 4. Let F and H be of the fame piece of wood as E and G, but as much thinner as poffible, to make the work light.

Sixth and Seventh Mutations.

The blocks of thefe 2 mutations are turned out of 1 piece of wood, whofe length from F to P is 15 inches. L, a block 5 inches diameter, in which are fixed 8 fpokes, each 2 foot 4 inches long; at the end of each fpoke tie 2 4 oz. cafes, as N°. 6. all thefe cafes muft be fired at the fame time, by a pipe brought from the end of one of the cafes on the 5th mutation. Let the diftance between the fpokes at L and thefe in the 5th mutation be 7 inches. M, the nave of the 7th mutation, whofe diameter muft be 5 ½ inches: in this nave fix 8 fpokes, and on the front of them 2 circular fells, 1 of 4 feet 8 inches diameter, and 1 of 3 feet 11 diameter; on thefe fells tie 1 6 8-oz. or pound cafes as in N°. 7. and carry leaders from one to the other, fo that they may be all fired together. This mutation muft be fired by a leader brought from the tail of one of the cafes on the fixth mutation.

Eighth and Ninth Mutations.

The blocks of thefe may be turned out of one piece, whofe length from P to D muft be 12 inches. O, the block of the 8th mutation, which muft be 6 inches diameter, and in it fixed 6 fpokes, each 3 feet in length, ftrengthened by an hexagon fell within 3 or 4 inches of the ends of the fpokes; clofe to the end of each fpoke, in the front, fix a five-pointed brilliant ftar; then 7 inches below each ftar, tie 2 10-inch 8-oz. cafes, fo that the upper ends of the cafes may reft on the fells, and their ends on the fpokes; each of thefe cafes muft be placed parallel to the oppofite fell. See N°. 8. NNN, &c. are the cafes, and kkk, &c. the ftars.

The

The 9th mutation is thus made. Let D be a block 7
inches diameter; in this block muſt be ſcrewed 6 ſpokes,
6 feet long each, with holes and grooves for leaders, as
thoſe in the dodecaedron; at the end of each ſpoke, in
the front, fix a ſpindle for a hexagon vertical wheel,
10 inches diameter, as in Nº. 9. When theſe wheels are
on, carry a leader from each into the block, ſo that they
may all meet; then lead a pipe from the end of 1 of the
caſes of the 8th mutation, through a hole bored in the
block D, to meet the leaders from the vertical wheels,
ſo that they may all be fired together.

The ſpindles for large pieces are required to be made
very ſtrong, and as exact as poſſible: for a piece of
9 mutations, let the ſpindle be at the large end 1 inch diameter, and continue that thickneſs as far as the 7th mutation, and from thence to the 5th; let its diameter be ¾ of
an inch; from the fifth to the fourth, 5 8ths of an inch;
from the fourth to the ſecond, ½ an inch; and from the
ſecond to the end, 3 8ths of an inch: at the ſmall end
muſt be a nut to keep on the firſt wheel, and at the thick
end muſt be a large nut, as ſhewn by the figure; ſo that
the ſcrew part of the ſpindle being put through a poſt, and
a nut ſcrewed on tight, the ſpindle will be held faſt and
ſteady; but you are to obſerve, that that part of the ſpindle, on which the moveable pieces are to run, be made
long enough for the wheels to run eaſy without ſticking;
the fixed pieces being made on different blocks, the leaders muſt be joined, after they are fixed on the ſpindle.
The beſt method of preventing the fixed mutations from
moving on the ſpindle, is, to make that part of the ſpindle which goes through them ſquare; but as it would be
difficult to make ſquare holes through ſuch long blocks
as are ſometimes required, it will be beſt to make them
thus : Bore a round hole a little larger than the diameter
of the ſpindle, and at each end of the block over the
hole, faſten a piece of braſs with a ſquare hole in it to
fit the ſpindle.

To make an Horizontal Wheel change to a Vertical Wheel with a Sun in Front.

The fudden change of this piece is very pleafing, and gives great furprife to thofe who are not acquainted with the contrivance. A wheel for this purpofe fhould be about 3 feet diameter, and its fell circular, on which tie 16 half-pound cafes filled with brilliant charge; 2 of thefe cafes muft burn at a time, and on each end of the nave muft be a tin barrel of the fame conftruction as thofe on the regulated piece; the wheel being completed, prepare the poft or ftand thus: firft have a ftand made of any height, about 3 or 4 inches fquare; then faw off from the top, a piece 2 feet long; this piece join again at the place where it was cut, with a hinge on one fide, fo that it may lift up and down in the front of the ftand, then fix on the top of the bottom part of the ftand, on each fide a bracket: thefe brackets muft project at right angles with the ftand, 1 foot from the front, for the fhort piece to reft on; but thefe brackets muft be placed a little above the joint of the poft, fo that when the upper ftand falls, it may lie between them at right angles with the bottom ftand, which may be done by fixing a piece of wood, 1 foot long, between the brackets, and even with the top of the bottom ftand; then, as the brackets rife above the bottom ftand, they will form a channel for the fhort poft to lie in, and keep it fteady without ftraining the hinge: on the fide of the fhort poft oppofite the hinge, nail a piece of wood, of fuch a length, that, when the poft is perpendicular, it may reach about $1\frac{1}{2}$ foot down the long poft, to which being tied, it will hold the fhort ftand upright: the ftand being thus prepared, in the top of it fix a fpindle 10 inches long; on this fpindle put the wheel, then fix on a brilliant fun with a fingle glory; the diameter of this fun muft be 6 inches lefs than that of the wheel. When you fire this piece, light the wheel firft, and let it

run

run horizontally till 4 cafes are confumed; then from the
end of the 4th cafe carry a leader into the tin barrel that
turns over the end of the ftand; this leader muft be met by
another brought through the top of the poft, from a cafe
filled with a ftrong port-fire charge, and tied to the bottom poft, with its mouth facing the pack-thread which
holds up the ftand, fo that when this cafe is lighted, it
will burn the pack-thread, and let the wheel fall forward,
by which means it will become vertical; then from the
laft cafe of the wheel, carry a leader into the barrel next
the fun, which will begin as foon as the wheel is burnt
out.

Grand Volute illuminated with a projected Wheel in Front.

Firft have 2 hoops made of ftrong iron wire, one of
6 feet diameter, and one of 4 feet 2 inches; thefe hoops
muft be joined to fcrolls A, A, A, &c. as in Fig. 54.
Thefe fcrolls muft be made of the fame fort of wire as the
hoops: on thefe fcrolls tie, with iron binding wire, as
many illuminating port-fires as they will hold, at 2 inches
diftance: thefe port fires clothe with leaders, fo that they
may all take fire together; then let C be a circular wheel
of 4 fpokes, 3 feet 6 inches diameter, and on its fell tie
as many 4 oz. cafes, head to tail, as will complete the
circle, only allowing a fufficient diftance between the
cafes, that the fire may pafs free, which may be done by
cutting the upper part of the end of each cafe a little fhelv-
ing: on each fpoke fix a 4 oz. cafe about 3 inches from
the fell of the wheel; thefe cafes are to burn one at a time,
and the firft of them to begin with thofe on the fell, of
which 4 are to burn at a time, fo that the wheel will laft no
longer than ¼ of the cafes on the fell, which in number
fhould be 16 or 20: on the front of the wheel form a fpiral
line, with ftrong wire, on which tie port fires, placing them
on a flant, with their mouths to face the fame way as the
cafes on the wheel; all thefe port fires muft be fired with the
2d cafes of wheel. Let D, D, D, &c. be fpokes of wood,
all made to fcrew into a block in the centre; each of thefe
fpokes

spokes may be in length about 4 feet 6 inches; in the top of each fix a spindle, and on each spindle put a spirali wheel of 8 spokes, such as E, E, E, &c. The blocks of these wheels must have a hole at top for the centre cases, and the spindle must have nuts screwed on their ends; which nuts should fit in the holes at top of the blocks, so so that all the wheels must be put on before you fix in the centre cases: as some of these wheels by reason of their situation will not bear on the nut, it will be necessary to have smooth shoulders made on the spindles for the blocks to run on; the cases of these wheels are to burn double, and the method of firing them is, by carrying a leader from each down the spokes into the block in the centre, as in the dodecaedron, but the centre case of each wheel must begin with the 2 last cases as usual. It is to be observed, that the large circular wheel in front must have a tin barrel on its block, into which a pipe must be carried from one of the second cases on the wheel; this pipe being met by another from the large block, in which the 8 spokes are screwed, will fire all the spirali wheels and the illuminating port fires at the same time. The cases of the projected wheel may be filled with a white charge, and those of the spirali wheels, with a grey.

Moon and Seven Stars.

Let Fig. 55. be a smooth circular board, 6 feet diameter; out of the middle of it cut a circular piece 12 or 14 inches diameter, and over the vacancy put white Persian silk, on which paint a moon's face; then let I, I, I, &c. be stars each 4 or 5 inches diameter, cut out with 5 points, and covered with oiled silk: on the front of the large circular board, draw a 7-pointed star, as large as the circle will allow; then on the lines which form this star, bore holes, wherein fix pointed stars. When this piece is to be fired, it must be fixed upon the front of a post, on a spindle, with a wheel of brilliant fire behind the face of the moon; so that while the wheel burns, the moon and stars will appear transparent, and when the wheel has burnt out, they will dis-

appear,

appear, and the large ftar in front, which is formed of pointed ftars, will begin, being lighted by a pipe of communication from the laft cafe of the vertical wheel, behind the moon; this pipe muft be managed in the fame manner as thofe in regulated pieces.

Double Cone Wheel Illuminated.

This piece is reprefented by Fig. 56. Let A be a ftrong decagon wheel, 2 feet 6 inches diameter; then on each fide of it fix a cone B and C; thefe cones are to confift of a number of hoops, fupported by 3 or 4 pieces of wood, in the manner of the fpiral wheels: let the height of each cone be 3 feet 6 inches, and on all the hoops tie port fires horizontally, with their mouths outwards, and clothe the wheel with 8 ounce cafes, all to play horizontally, 2 at a time: the cones may be fired with the firft or fecond cafes. The fpindle for this piece muft go through both the cones, and rife 3 feet above the point of the cone at top, fo that its length will be 10 feet 4 inches from the top of the poft H, in which it is fixed, allowing 4 inches for the thicknefs of the block of the wheel: the whole weight of the wheel and cones muft bear on a fhoulder in the fpindle, on which the block of the wheel muft turn: near the top of the fpindle muft be a hole in the front, into which fcrew a fmall fpindle, after the cones are on; then on this fmall fpindle fix a fun, D, compofed of 16 nine-inch 4 oz. cafes, of brilliant fire; which cafes muft not be placed on a fell, but only ftuck into a block of 6 inches diameter: then in the front of this fun muft be a circular vertical wheel, 16 inches diameter; on the front of this wheel form with iron wire a fpiral line, and clothe it with illuminations, after the ufual method. As this wheel is not to be fired till the cones are burnt out, the method of firing it is,—Let the hole in the block, at the top of the uppermoft cone, be a little larger than the fpindle which paffes through it, then, from the firft cafe of the vertical wheel before the fun, carry a leader down the fide of the fpindle to the top

of the block of the horizontal wheel, on which muſt be
a tin barrel; then this leader, being met by another
brought from the end of the laſt caſe of the horizontal
wheel, will give fire to the vertical wheel, ſo ſoon as the
cones are extinguiſhed; but the ſun, D, muſt not be
fired, till the vertical wheel is quite burnt out.

Fire-Pumps.

Caſes for fire-pumps are made as thoſe for tourbillons;
only they are paſted, inſtead of being rolled dry. Having rolled and dried your caſes, fill them: firſt put in a
little meal powder, and then a ſtar; on which ram lightly
a ladle or 2 of compoſition, then a little meal powder,
and on that a ſtar, then again compoſition, and ſo on till
you have filled the caſe. Stars for fire-pumps ſhould
not be round, but muſt be made either ſquare, or flat and
circular, with a hole through the middle: the quantity
of powder for throwing the ſtars muſt increaſe as you
come near the top of the caſe; for, if much powder be
put at the bottom, it will burſt the caſe. The ſtars muſt
differ in ſize, in this manner: let the ſtar which you put
in firſt, be about ¼ leſs than the bore of the caſe; but let
the next ſtar be a little larger, and the 3d ſtar a little
larger than the 2d, and ſo on: let them increaſe in diameter, till within 2 of the top of the caſe, which 2 muſt
fit in tight. As the loading of fire-pumps is ſomewhat
difficult, it will be neceſſary to make 2 or 3 trials, before
you depend on their performance: when you fill a number of pumps, take care not to put in each an equal quantity of charge between the ſtars, ſo that when they are
fired they may not throw up too many ſtars together.
Caſes for fire-pumps ſhould be made very ſtrong, and
rolled on 4 or 8 oz. formers, 10 or 12 inches long each.

Vertical Scroll Wheel.

This wheel may be made of any diameter, but muſt
be conſtructed as in Fig. 57, to do which proceed thus:
Have a block made of a moderate ſize, into which fix
4 flat ſpokes, and on them fix a flat circular fell of wood;
round the front of this fell place port-fires; then on the
front of the ſpokes form a ſcroll, either with a hoop or
ſtrong iron wire; on this ſcroll tie caſes of brilliant fire,
in proportion to the wheel, head to tail, as in the figure.
When you fire this wheel, light the firſt caſe near the fell;
then, as the caſes fire ſucceſſively, you will ſee the circle
of fire gradually diminiſh; but whether the illuminations
on the fell begin with the ſcroll, or not, is immaterial,
that being left intirely to the maker.

N. B. This wheel may be put in the front of a regulated piece, or fired by itſelf, occaſionally.

Pin-Wheels.

Firſt roll ſome paper pipes, about 14 inches long each:
theſe pipes muſt not be made thick of paper, 2 or 3 rounds
of elephant paper being ſufficient. When your pipes are
thoroughly dried, you muſt have made a tin tube, 12 inches
long, to fit eaſy into the pipes; at one end of this tube fix
a ſmall conical cup, which done is called a funnel: then
bend 1 end of 1 of the pipes, and put the funnel in at the
other, as far as it will reach, and fill the cup with compoſition: then draw out the funnel by a little at a time,
ſhaking it up and down; and it will fill the pipe as it
comes out. Having filled ſome pipes, have made ſome
ſmall blocks, about 1 inch diameter, and ½ inch thick:
round 1 of theſe blocks wind and paſte a pipe, and to
the end of this pipe join another; which muſt be done by
twiſting the end of one pipe to a point, and putting it
into the end of the other, with a little paſte: in this manner join 4 or 5 pipes, winding them one upon the other,
ſo as to form a ſpiral line. Having wound on your pipes,

paſte

pafte 2 flips of paper acrofs them, to hold them together: befides thefe flips of paper the pipes muft be
pafted together.

There is another method of making thefe wheels, called
the French; which is, by winding on the pipes without
pafte, and fticking them together with fealing-wax, at
every half-turn; fo that, when they are fired, the end
will fall loofe every time the fire paffes the wax; by
which means the circle of fire will be confiderably increafed. The formers for thefe pipes are made from
1 ½ to 4 16ths of an inch diameter, and the compofition
for them as follows; meal powder 8 oz. faltpetre 2 oz.
and fulphur 1: among thefe ingredi nts may be mixed a
little fteel-filings, or the duft of caft iron: this compofition fhould be very dry, and not made too fine, or it will
ftick in the funnel. Thefe wheels may be fired on a
large pin, and held in the hand with fafety.

Fire-Globes.

There are 2 forts of fire globes, one with projected
cafes, the other with the cafes concealed thus: Have a
globe made of wood, of any diameter you chufe, and
divide the furface of it into 14 equal parts, and at each
divifion bore a hole perpendicular to the centre: thefe
holes muft be in proportion to the cafes intended to be
ufed: in every hole, except one, put a cafe filled with
brilliant, or any other charge, and let the mouths of the
cafes be even with the furface of the globe; then cut in
the globe a groove, from the mouth of one cafe to the
other, for leaders, which muft be carried from cafe to
cafe, fo that they may all be fired together: this
done, cover the globe with a fingle paper, and paint
it. Thefe globes may be ufed to ornament a building.

Fire-globes with projected cafes are made thus: Your
globe being made with 14 holes bored in it as ufual, fix
in every hole, except one, a cafe, and let each cafe project from the globe 2 thirds of its length; then clothe
all the cafes with leaders, fo that they may all take fire

at

at the fame time. Fire-globes are fupported by a pintle made to fit the hole in which there is no cafe.

To thread and join Leaders, and place them on different Works.

Joining and placing Leaders is a very effential part of fire-works, as it is on the leaders that the performance of all complex works depends; for which reafon I fhall endeavour here to explain the method of conducting pipes of communication, in as plain a manner as poffible. Your works being ready to be clothed, proceed thus: Cut your pipes of a fufficient length to reach from one cafe to the other; then put in the quick-match, which muft always be made to go in very eafy: when the match is in, cut it off within about an inch of the end of the pipe, and let it project as much at the other end; then faften the pipe to the mouth of each cafe with a pin, and put the loofe ends of the match into the mouths of the cafes, with a little meal powder: this done to all the cafes, pafte over the mouth of each 2 or 3 bits of paper. The preceding method is ufed for large cafes, and the following for fmall, and for illuminations: Firft thread a long pipe; then lay it on the tops of the cafes, and cut a bit off the under fide, over the mouth of each cafe, fo that the match may appear; then pin the pipe to every other cafe, but before you put on the pipes, put a little meal powder in the mouth of each cafe: if the cafes thus clothed are port fires on illuminated works, cover the mouth of each cafe with a fingle paper; but, if they are choaked cafes, fitu-ated fo that a number of fparks from other works may fall on them before they are fired, fecure them with 3 or 4 papers, which muft be pafted on very fmooth, that there may be no creafes for the fparks to lodge in, which oft fet fire to the works before their time. Avoid, as much as poffible, placing the leaders too near, or one acrofs the other fo as to touch, as it may happen that the flafh of one will fire the other; therefore, if your works fhould be fo formed, that the leaders muft crofs or touch, be fure

K to

to make them very strong, and secure at the joints, and at every opening.

When a great length of pipe is required, it must be made by joining several pipes in this manner: Having put on 1 length of match as many pipes as it will hold, paste paper over every joint; but, if a still greater length is required, more pipes must be joined, by cutting off about an inch of one side of each pipe near the end, and laying the quick-match together, and tying them fast with small twine; after which, cover the joining with pasted paper.

Placing Fire-works to be exhibited, with the Order of Firing.

Nothing adds more to the appearance of fire-works, than the placing them properly; though the manner of placing them chiefly depends on the judgement of the maker. I shall give such rules here, as have been generally observed; for example, whether your works are to be fired on a building, or on stands: If they are a double set, place one wheel of a sort on each side of the building; and next to each of them, towards the centre, place a fixed piece, then wheels, and so on; leaving a sufficient distance between them, for the fire to play from one without burning the other: Having fixed some of your works thus in front, place the rest behind them, in the centre of their intervals: the largest piece, which is generally a regulated or transparent piece, must be placed in the centre of the building, and behind it a sun, which must always stand above all the other works: a little before the building, or stands, place your large gerbes; and at the back of the works, fix your marron batteries, pots des aigrettes, pots des brins, pots des saucissons, air ballóons, and flights of rockets: the rocket stands may be fixed behind, or any where else, so as not to be in the way of the works.

Single

Single collections are fired on stands; which stands are made in the same manner as theodolite stands, only the top part must be long or short occasionally: these stands may be fixed up very soon without much trouble. Having given sufficient instructions for placing of fireworks, I shall proceed with the manner of firing them.

Order of Firing.

1. Two signal ⎫
2. Six sky ⎪ rockets
3. Two honorary ⎬
4. Four caduceus ⎭

5. ⎫ ⎧ vertical ⎫
6. ⎬ Two ⎨ spiral ⎬ wheels illuminated
7. ⎭ ⎩ transparent stars ⎭

8. A line rocket of 5 changes
9. Four tourbillons

10. ⎫ ⎧ horizontal wheels
11. ⎪ ⎪ air balloons illuminated
12. ⎬ Two ⎨ Chinese fountains
13. ⎪ ⎪ regulating pieces of 4 mutations each
14. ⎭ ⎩ pots des aigrettes

15. Three large gerbes
16. A flight of rockets

17. ⎫ Two ⎧ balloon wheels
18. ⎭ ⎩ cascades of brilliant fire

19. Twelve sky rockets

20. ⎫ Two ⎧ illuminated yew trees
21. ⎭ ⎩ air balloons of serpents, and 2 compound

22. Four tourbillons

23. ⎫ Two ⎧ Fruiloni wheels
24. ⎭ ⎩ illuminated globes with horizontal wheels

25. One pot des sauciffons
26. Two plural wheels
27. Marron battery
28. Two chandeliers illuminated
29. Range of pots des brins

30. Twelve

30. Twelve sky rockets
31. Two yew-trees of fire
32. Nest of serpents
33. Two double cones illuminated
34. Regulating piece of seven mutations, viz.
     1. Vertical wheel illuminated
     2. Golden glory
     3. Octagon vertical wheel
     4. Porcupine's quills
     5. Cross fires
     6 Star piece with brilliant rays
     7. Six vertical wheels
35. Brilliant sun
36. Large flight of rockets.

When water-works are to be exhibited, divide them into several sets, and fire one set after every fifth or sixth change of land and air-works. Observe this rule in firing a double set of works; always to begin with sky-rockets, then two moveable pieces; then two fixed pieces, and so on; ending with a large flight of rockets, or a marron battery: if a single collection, fire a fixed piece after every wheel or two, and now and then some air and water-works.

Fountain of Sky Rockets.

Plate 6th, Fig. 1. represents a fountain of 30 rockets. Let A be a perpendicular post, 16 feet high from the ground, and 4 inches square. Let the rail, or cross piece, C, be 1 foot 6 inches long, 3 inches broad, and 1 thick. The rail D, at bottom, must be 6 feet long, 1 foot broad, and 1 inch thick. F, and G, are the two sides which serve to supply the rails D, E, H, I, C: these sides are 1 foot broad at bottom, and cut in the front with a regular slope, to 3 inches at top; but their back edges must be parallel with the front of the pots A. The breadth of the rails E, H, I, will be determined by the breadth of the sides: all the rails must be fixed at 2 feet diftance from each other, and at right angles with the pots. Having placed the rails thus, bore in the bottom rail 10 holes, at equal diftances, large enough to receive the ftick of a one-pound rocket; in the back edge of this rail cut a groove from one end to the other, fit to contain a quick-match; then cut a groove in the top of the rail, from the edge of each hole, into the groove in the back: in the fame manner cut in the fecond rail, E, 8 holes and grooves; in the third rail, H, 6 holes and grooves; in the fourth rail, I, 4 holes and grooves; and in the top rail, 2 holes and grooves. B, a rail with holes in it to guide the ends of the rocket fticks: this rail muft be fixed 6 feet from the rail D. The fountain frame being thus made, prepare your rockets thus: Tie round the mouth of each a piece of thin paper, large enough to go twice round, and to projeCt about an inch and ¼ from the mouth of the rocket, which muft be rubbed with wet meal-powder; in the mouth of each rocket put a leader, which fecure well with the paper that projeCts from the mouth of the cafe: thefe leaders muft be carried into the grooves in the back of the rails, in which lay a quick-match from one end to the other, and cover it with pafted paper: holes muft be made in the rail D, to receive the ends of the fticks of the rockets, in the rail E, and fo on to the fourth rail; fo that the fticks of the rockets at top will go through all the rails. The rockets being fo prepared, fix a gerbe, or white flower pot, on each rail, before the poft, with their mouths inclining a little forwards: thefe gerbes muft be lighted all at once. Behind or before each gerbe, fix a cafe of brilliant or flow fire: thefe cafes muft be filled fo that they may burn out one after the other, to regulate the fountain, which may be done by carrying a leader, from the end of each flow or brilliant fire, into the groove in the back of each rail. Different fized rockets may be ufed in thefe fountains; but it will be beft to fill the heads of the rockets on each rail with different forts of things, in this manner; thofe at top with crackers, the next with rains, the third with

K 3   ferpents,

ferpents, the fourth with tailed ftars, and the laft flight with common or brilliant ftars.

Palm-Tree.

This piece, though made of common fires, and of a fimple conftruction, has a very pleafing effect; owing to the fires interfecting fo oft, that they refemble the branches of trees. Fig. 2d. Let o be a perpendicular poft, of any thicknefs, fo that it is fufficiently ftrong to hold the cafes: let the diftance from B to C be 2 feet 6 inches, and from C to D 2 feet 6 inches; and let the length of each crofs piece be 2 feet, on each end of each fix a five-pointed ftar; then fix on pegs made on purpofe, 12 inch half-pound cafes of brilliant fire, as in the figure. All the cafes and ftars muft be fired at once. This piece fhould be fixed high from the ground.

Illuminated Pyramid, with Archimedian Screws, a Globe and Vertical Sun,

May be made of any fize: one made according to the dimenfions of Fig. 3d, will be a good proportion, whofe height is 21 feet; from C to D, 6 feet; from E to F, 9 feet: the fpace between the rails muft be 6 inches, and the rails as thin as poffible: in all the rails ftick port-fires at 4 inches diftance. The Archimedian fcrews, G, K, are nothing more than double fpiral wheels, with the cafes placed on their wheels horizontally, inftead of obliquely. The vertical fun, I, need not confift of more than 12 rays, to form a fingle glory. The globe at top muft be made in proportion to the pyramid, which being prepared according to the preceding directions, place your leaders fo that all the illuminating port-fires, fcrews, globe, and fun, may take fire together. The pyramid muft be fupported by the 2 fides, and by a fupport brought from a pole, which muft be placed 2 feet from the back of the pyramid, that the wheels may run free,

Rofe

Rofe-Piece and Sun.

A rofe-piece may be ufed for a mutation of a regulated piece, or fired by itfelf: it makes the beft appearance when made large; if its exterior diameter be 6 feet, it will be a good fize. Fig. 4. fhews the manner it appears in before it is fired. Let the exterior fell be made of wood, and fupported by 4 wooden fpokes; all the other parts, on which the illuminations are fixed, muft be made of ftrong iron wire: on the exterior fell place as many $\frac{1}{2}$lb. cafes of brilliant charge as you think proper, but the more the better ; for the nearer the cafes are placed, the ftronger will be the rays of the fun: the illuminations fhould be placed within 3 inches of each other ; they muft be all fired together, and burn fome time before the fun is lighted ; which may be done by carrying a leader from the middle of one of the illuminations, to the mouth of one of the fun cafes.

Tranfparent Stars with Illuminated Rays,

Plate 7, Fig. 5th, reprefents an illuminated ftar. Let the diameter from A to B be 2 feet, and from C to D, 7 feet. Firft make a ftrong circular back or body of the ftar, 2 feet diameter, to which you fix the illuminated rays : in the centre of the front of the body fix a fpindle, on which put a double triangular wheel, 6 inches diameter, clothed with 2 ounce cafes of brilliant charge ; the cafes on this wheel muft burn but 1 at time. Round the edge of the body nail a hoop made of thin wood or tin : this hoop muft project in front 6 or 7 inches : in this hoop cut 3 or 4 holes to let out the fmoke from the wheel. The ftar and garter may be cut out of ftrong pafte-board, or tin, made in this manner : cut a round piece of pafteboard, or tin, 2 feet diameter, on which draw a ftar, and cut it out; then over the vacancy pafte Perfian filk ; paint the letters yellow ; 4 of the rays yellow, and 4 red ; the crofs in the middle may be painted half red, and half yellow, or yellow and blue. This

K 4 tranfparent

tranfparent ftar muft be faftened to the wooden hoop by a fcrew, to take off and on : the illuminated rays are made of thin wood, with tin fockets fixed on their fides within 4 inches of each other; in thefe fockets ftick illuminating port-fires; behind the point of each ray fix a half-pound cafe of grey, black, or Chinefe fire.

N. B. The illuminated rays to be lighted at the fame time as the triangular wheel, or after it is burnt out; which may be done by a tin barrel being fixed to the wheel, after the manner of thofe in the regulated pieces. Into this barrel carry a leader from the illuminated rays, through the back of the ftar; which leader muft be met by another, brought from the tail of the laft cafe on the wheel.

Tranfparent Table Star illuminated.

Fig. 6th reprefents a table ftar, whofe diameter, from E to F, is 12 feet; and from E to I, 4. This proportion, obferved on each fide, will make the centre frame 4 feet fquare: in this fquare fix a tranfparent ftar, as in the figure. This ftar may be painted blue, and its rays made as thofe of the flaming ftars defcribed in page 113. The wheel for this ftar may be compofed of different coloured fires, with a change or 2 of flow fire: the wheels a, a, a, a, may be clothed with any number of cafes, fo that the ftar wheel confifts of the fame: the illuminating portfires, which muft be placed very near each other on the frames, muft be fo managed as to burn as long as the wheels, and lighted at the time.

The Regulated Illuminated Spirali Piece, with a projected Star Wheel illuminated.

This piece is reprefented by Fig. 7. and is thus made. Have a block made 8 inches diameter; in this block fcrew 6 iron fpokes, which muft ferve for fpindles for the fpiral wheels: thefe wheels are made as ufual, each 1 foot

6 diameter,

6 diameter, and 3 feet in height: the fpindles muft be long enough to keep the wheels 4 or 5 inches from one another: at the end of each fpindle muft be a fcrew nut, on which the wheels that hang downwards will run; and on the fpindles which ftand upwards muft be a fhoulder, for the blocks of the wheels to run on.

The projected ftar-wheel muft turn on the fame fpindle on which the large block is fixed: this fpindle muft be long enough to allow the ftar-wheel to project a little before the fpiral wheels: the exterior diameter of the ftar-wheel muft be 3 feet 5. On this wheel fix 3 circles of iron wire, and on them port-fires; on the block place a tranfparent ftar, or a large 5-pointed brilliant ftar. The cafes on this wheel may burn 4 at once, as it will contain near twice the number of one of the fpiral wheels: the cafes on the fpiral wheels muft be placed parallel to their fells, and burn 2 at a time.

A New Figure-Piece illuminated with Five-Pointed Stars.

The conftruction of this piece is very eafy, as fhewn by Fig. 8, whofe diameter from B to C is 8 feet, and from D to E 2 feet: the vertical wheel in the centre muft be 1 foot diameter, and confift of 6 four-ounce cafes of different coloured charge, which cafes muft burn double: on the frames fix 5-pointed brilliant or blue ftars, rammed 4 inches with compofition: let the fpace between each ftar be 8 inches; at each point fix a gerbe, or cafe of Chinefe fire. When to be fired, let the gerbes, ftars, and wheel, be lighted at the fame time.

The Star-Wheel Illuminated.

This beautiful new-invented piece is fhewn in Plate 8, Fig. 9. its exterior fell is made of wood, 3 feet 6, or 4 feet diameter: within this fell, form with iron wire 3 circles, one lefs than the other, fo that the diameter of the leaft

may

may be about 10 inches: place the port-fires on thefe fells with their mouths inclining outwards, and the port-fires on the points of the ftar with their mouths projecting in front: let the exterior fell be clothed with 4-ounce cafes of grey charge: thefe cafes muft burn 4 at a time, and be lighted at the fame time as the illuminations.

Pyramid of Flower-Pots.

Fig. 10. reprefents this curious piece, which muft be made thus. Let the diftance from A to B be 6 feet, and from one rail to the other 2: on the bottom rail fix 5 paper mortars, each 3½ inches diameter: thefe mortars load with ferpents, crackers, ftars, &c.

In the centre of each mortar fix a cafe of fpur-fire: on the fecond rail fix 4 mortars, fo as to ftand exactly in the middle of the intervals of them on the bottom rail; on the third rail place 3 mortars; on the fourth, 2; and on the top of the pofts, 1: the bottom rail muft be 6 feet long: all the mortars muft incline a little forwards, that they may eafily difcharge; and the fpur-fires rammed exactly alike, that the mortars may all be fired at the fame time. Having prepared your pyramid according to the preceding directions, carry pipes of communication from one fpur-fire to the other.

The illuminated Regulating Piece.

Fig. 11. reprefents one half of this piece. A, A, A, A, are flat wooden fpokes, each 5 feet long; and at the end of each place a vertical wheel, 10 inches diameter, clothed with 6 4-ounce cafes of brilliant fire: thefe cafes muft burn but 1 at a time: on 2 of the fpokes of each wheel place 2 port-fires, which muft be lighted with the firft cafe of the wheel; on each fpoke A, A, &c. behind the wheels, place 6 cafes of the fame fize as them on the wheels: thefe cafes muft be tied acrofs the fpokes with their mouths all one way, and be made to take fire fucceffively one after the other, fo that they may affift the whole pieces to turn round,

The

The diameter of the wheel B muſt be 2 feet 6, and its fell made of wood, which muſt be fixed to the large ſpokes: on this wheel place 24 caſes of the ſame ſort as them on the ſmall wheels; theſe caſes muſt burn 4 at a time: in this wheel make 3 circles with iron wire, and on them place illuminating port-fires, as in the figure: the ſtar points on the large ſpokes may be made of thin aſh-hoops; the diameter of theſe points cloſe to the centre wheel muſt be 11 inches: on theſe points place port-fires, at 3½ inches diſtance one from the other.

Fig. 12. repreſents the blocks of this piece. The diameters of theſe blocks, at A and B, muſt be 8 inches; and C and D, 4½ inches: the length of each of theſe blocks muſt be 6 inches: at the ſmall ends of theſe blocks fix an iron wheel 5 inches diameter, which wheels muſt have teeth, to turn the wheel E: this wheel is fixed on a ſmall ſpindle ſcrewed into the large ſpindle, which goes through the two blocks, and on which they run.

Suppoſing Fig. 11. to be on the block A, in Fig. 12, and to turn to the right, and another piece of the ſame conſtruction on the block B, with its fires placed ſo as to turn it to the left; you will find them move very true and faſt, by the help of the 3 iron wheels, which ſerve to regulate their motions, as well as to aſſiſt them in turning: let the iron circles in the front of the great wheels be of different diameters, ſo that when fired there may appear 6 circles. When this piece is fired, all the wheels and illuminations muſt be lighted at one time.

To fix a Sky-Rocket with its Stick on the Top of another.

Rockets thus managed make a pretty appearance, by reaſon of a freſh tail being ſeen when the ſecond rocket takes fire, which will mount to a great height. The method of preparing theſe rockets is thus: Having filled a two-pounder, which muſt be filled only half a diameter above the piercer, and in its head not more than 10 or 12 ſtars;

the

the ftick of this rocket .muft be made a little thicker than common, and when made, cut it in half the flat way, and in each half make a groove, fo that, when the 2 halves are joined, the hollow made by the grooves may be large enough to hold the ftick of a half-pound rocket; which rocket make and head as ufual; the ftick of this rocket put into the hollow of the large one, fo far that the mouth of the rocket may reft on the head of the two-pounder; from whofe head carry a leader into the mouth of the fmall rocket; which being done, your rockets will be ready for firing.

A New Method of Placing Leaders.

The placing leaders on fmall cafes, or illuminations, is a much quicker, ftronger, and more expeditious way than that of ufing pins; which method has been practifed till lately. Your port-fires being filled within about 3 8ths of an inch of the top, bore with an awl a hole thro' each fide of the cafe, clofe to the compofition; then fill the mouths of the cafes with meal powder wetted with fpirit of wine: when you have thus prepared your cafes, fix them on your works; then take an empty leader, and lay it on the mouths of as many cafes as it will reach; then, with your finger nail, mark the leader exactly in the middle of the mouth of each cafe; then at each mark, with a pair of fciffars, cut a bit out of the pipe, fo that, when you put in the quick-match, it may be feen. This done, lay the leader on the cafes again, with that fide on which the match is feen downwards; then take fome fmall twine, and put it through the holes in the mouths of the cafes, and tie on the leader: do this to every cafe, and cover them with fingle pafted paper. By making ufe of this method your works may be made very clean, there being no occafion to put dry meal powder in the mouths of the cafes, which always foils the works, and prevents the pafte from fticking.

Here

Here I have taught the method of rolling, pinching, and filling all sorts of cases; the manner of pulverizing, mixing, and preparing, all compositions used in artificial fire-works; also the method of placing leaders, clothing wheels, fixed pieces, &c. in so plain a manner, that all fire-works may be made without any further instructions. A variety of pyrotechnical representations only depends on the genius of the maker, by fixing different cases and fires on works of various forms, of which there are many more.

But as those I have given are the principal, I shall conclude with Mr. Muller's Laboratory and a few of his Mines; which are all that was wanting to complete this work.

Mr. MULLER on LABORATORY WORKS.

MY defign is not to give here any more than what is juft neceffary for the young Artillerift to know in the courfe of his duty, referring that part which regards the Fire-works made for Rejoicing to the excellent Treatife on Artificial Fireworks, wrote by *Robert Jones*, who gives all that can be faid on that fubject, and has himfelf practifed every part of it.

Grapefhot.

The number of fhot in a grape varies according to the fervice or fize of the guns: in fea-fervice 9 is always the number; but by land it is increafed to any number or fize; from an ounce and a quarter in weight, to 3 or 4 pounds. It has not been determined, what number or fize anfwers beft in practice; which I think fhould be tried: for it is well known, that they oft fcatter fo much, that only a fmall number take place. It would not be a ufelefs experiment, to try at what diftance they would do moft execution, and what is the beft charge of powder. In fea-fervice, the bottoms and pins are made of iron, whereas thofe ufed by land are of wood: for what reafon this diftinction is made, I cannot tell, unlefs that thefe iron bottoms are fuppofed to deftroy the riggings of fhips more than the wooden.

To make grape-fhot, a bag of coarfe cloth is made juft to hold the bottom which is put into it; then as many fhot as the grape is to contain; and with a ftrong packthread they are quilted to keep the fhot from moving, and when they are finifhed are put into boxes for carriage. When the fhot are fmall, they are put into tin boxes that fit the bore of the gun. Leaden bullets are likewife ufed

in

in the fame manner. It muft be obferved, that whatever number or fizes of the fhots are ufed, they muft weigh with their bottoms and pins nearly as much as the fhot of the piece.

Cartridges.

The loading and firing guns with cartridges is done much fooner, and lefs liable to accidents, than with loofe powder. They are made of various fubftances, fuch as paper, flannel, parchment, and bladders. When they are made of paper, the bottoms remain in the piece, and accumulate fo much, that the priming cannot reach the powder; and therefore they muft be drawn from time to time, which retards the fervice. They have another inconveniency, which is, they retain the fire; and, if particular care is not taken in fpunging the piece, they will fet fire to the next cartridge, and the gunner that puts it into the piece will be in danger of lofing a hand or arm, as has fometimes happened. When they are made of parchment or bladders, the fire fhrivels them up, whereby they enter into the vent, and become fo hard, that the priming iron cannot remove them fo as to clear the vent. Nothing has been found hitherto to anfwer better than flannel, and is the only thing ufed at prefent, becaufe it does not keep fire, and therefore not liable to accidents in the loading; but as the duft of powder paffes through them, a parchment cap is made to cover them, which is taken off before this is put into the piece.

The beft way of making flannel cartridges is, in my opinion, to boil the flannel in fize; this will prevent the duft of the powder from paffing through them, and renders them ftiff, and more manageable; for without this precaution they are fo pliable, that when they are large, and contain much powder, they are very inconvenient in putting them into the piece. The Saxon, who introduced our prefent light field pieces, had a particular method of preparing cartridges, which was fuch, that when laid into the fire they would not burn; and yet, by dipping them

into

into water before they were put into the piece, would take fire as quick as powder; but how he did it, nobody could tell; for he would not part with his secret.

In quick firing the shot is fixed to the cartridge by means of a wooden bottom, hollowed on one side so as to receive nearly half the shot, which is fastened to it by two small slips of tin crossing over the shot, and nailed to the bottom; and the cartridge is tied to the other end of this bottom. They are fixed likewise in the same manner to the bottoms of the grapeshot, which are used in field pieces.

Portfires.

Portfires are used sometimes instead of matches, to set fire to powder or compositions; and are distinguished into wet and dry. The composition of wet portfires is, saltpetre 4, sulphur 1, and mealed powder 4; when the composition is well mixed and sieved, it is to be moistened with a little linseed oil, and well rubbed with the hands till all the oil is well mixed with the composition. The composition of dry portfire is, saltpetre 4, sulphur 1, mealed powder 2, and antimony 1. These compositions are drove into small paper cases, and so kept till used.

Quickmatch

Is made with three cotton strands drawn into length, and put into a kettle covered with white wine vinegar, and a quantity of saltpetre and mealed powder, and boiled till well mixed. Others put only saltpetre into the water. After that, it is taken out hot, and laid in a trough where some mealed powder, moistened with spirits of wine, is thoroughly wrought into the cotton, by rolling it backwards and forwards with the hands: when this is done, they are taken out separately, and drawn through mealed powder, then hung upon a line till dry.

Tubes

Tubes ufed in quick Firing.

Thefe tubes are here made of tin: their diameter is two tenths of an inch, to enter into the vent of the piece; about 5 or 6 inches long, with a cap above, and cut flanting below in the form of a pen; and the point is ftrengthened with fome folder, that it may pierce the car-tridge. Through this tube is drawn a quickmatch, and the cap is filled with mealed powder moiftened with fpirit of wine. To prevent the mealed powder from falling out by carriage, a cap of paper is tied over it, which is taken off when ufed; but latterly this cap is made of flannel fteeped in fpirits of wine, with faltpetre diffolved in it; there is no occafion to take it off, fince it takes fire as quick as loofe powder.

An objection is made againft thefe tubes, which is, that the tin is apt to fpoil the quickmatch when they are kept for fome time; and it is imagined, that falt water would foon corrode them, therefore not proper to be ufed on board of fhips; this however has not been tried. The French ufe a fmall reed, to which is fixed a wooden cap about two inches long, filled with mealed powder moiftened with fpirit of wine: a fmall hole is made through them the fize of a needle, through which the fire darts with great violence, and gives fire to the cartridge, which muft be pierced with the priming iron. Thefe tubes may be kept a great while without being fpoiled; but the piercing the cartridge retards the quicknefs of firing. The forementioned Saxon made his of copper, tapering towards the end, fo as to enter the vent about half an inch, which is made fo far in the fame form, and the reft very narrow: they are filled in the fame manner as the French, and when fired, the flame darted through the cartridge without being pierced.

Fuzes for Shells and Hand-Grenades.

The compofition for fuzes is faltpetre 3, fulphur 1, and mealed powder 3, 4, and fometimes 5, according as required to burn quicker. Fuzes are chiefly made of very dry beech wood, and fometimes of hornbeam taken near the root; the upper part of that wood fplits very eafily. They are turned rough, and bored at firft, and then kept for feveral years in a dry place: the diameter of the hole is about a quarter of an inch, a little more or lefs is of no confequence; the hole does not go quite through, leaving about a quarter of an inch at the bottom; and the head is made hollow in the form of a bowl. The compofition is drove in with an iron driver, whofe ends are capped with copper to prevent the compofition from taking fire; and equally hard as poffible; the laft fhovel-full being all mealed powder, and two ftrands of quickmatch laid acrofs each other being drove in with it, the ends of which are folded up into the bowl, and a cap of parchment tied over it till ufed. Obferve, that, when fhells are to be thrown at a fmall diftance, the compofition fhould be made quicker than when they are to be thrown at a greater; for, by cutting them fo as to burn but a fhort time, they might not be long enough to be well fixed into the fhell, by which the blaft of the powder in the chamber would blow them out, without the fhell being able to burft. It muft likewife be obferved, that the cuftom of fixing the fhells at home is very bad, fince it is not known how long they fhould burn; and if they do not burft as foon as they fall, the execution is but trifling. Another difadvantage attends this practice; when they are carried into a hot climate the wood fhrinks, though ever fo dry before; and the fuzes loofen fo much, that they fall out in the flight of the fhell before it falls to the ground.

When the fuzes are to be drove, the lower end is cut off in a flope, fo as the compofition may give fire to the powder; and they muft have fuch a length, as to burft nearly as foon as the fhell touches the ground. When

the

the diftance of the battery from the object is known, the time of the fhell's flight may be computed nearly; which being known, the fuze may be cut accordingly, by burning 2 or 3, and making ufe of a watch, or a ftring by way of a pendulum.

Before fhells are loaded, they muft be well fearched within and without by means of a copper grater, to fee if there are no holes or cavities in them; after that put them into a tub of water, to cover them, with an empty fuze drove into them; and the mouth of a bellows, being introduced into the fuze, and worked, will caufe bubbles in the water, if there are any holes in the fhell; but if no bubbles appear, it is a fign the fhell is found and fit for fervice.

When loaded, care muft be taken that they are very dry within; and if the fpike which fupports the corp when they are caft, and which remains in them, is not beat down, it muft be done then, otherwife it would fplit the fuze. Then the powder is put into it with a funnel, and not quite filled, that the fuze may have room to enter, which fuze is preffed in at firft by the hand as far as it will go, and then drove with a mallet as hard as poffible, taking care not to fplit it; for if the leaft crack was in it, the compofition would give fire to the powder, and the fhell burft either in the mortar or the air, and do no execution.

It is a query how much powder is to be put into a fhell, fo as to make it burft in moft pieces. It is agreed by moft officers that they fhould not be quite filled; one that has taken moft pains to find it out, is of opinion that they fhould be filled within one third part of what they can hold.

Lieutenant Pirle, a very ingenious mechanic, loft in the Dodington fome years ago going to the Eaft-Indies, had found out a method, fo that as foon as the fhell touched the ground it burfted; but being too modeft a man, had not the affurance to propofe it to the mafter general of the ordnance, whereby the world was deprived of a moft ufeful invention.

L 2   If

If the fuzes are to be kept for some time after they are drove, the top must be covered with a mixture of pitch 2, rosin 1, and bees wax 3, whereby no air can come to the composition; and it will keep as long as you please.

Carcasses.

None but round carcasses are used at present, the flight of the oblong are so uncertain, that they are quite laid aside. The composition is pitch 2, saltpetre 4, sulphur 1, and corned powder 3. When the pitch is melted, the pot is taken off, and the ingredients well mixed put in; then the carcass is filled with as much as can be pressed in.

Light Balls to discover the Enemy's Works.

There are various sorts described. Some made of tow dipped into a composition of sulphur, pitch, rosin, and turpentine; and worked up into a ball. Others take a ball of stone or iron, which is covered with several coats of composition, much like that before mentioned, till of a proper size; the last coat is to be of grained powder. But the best sort, in my opinion, is to make a shell of paper the size of the mortar, and to fill it with a composition of an equal quantity of sulphur, pitch, rosin, and mealed powder; which being well mixed, and put in warm, will give a clear fire, and burn a considerable time.

There are many more things used in the defence of a breach; such as sacks filled with powder, bottles, barrels, &c. but as the chief intent of all these is to set fire, and blow up the assailants, and which every military gentleman may easily execute, we shall say no more here about them; our design being to instruct the young artillerist in the essential parts of his business; and to make him master of these matters, he must work in the laboratory; for practice is the best master.

Fireship,

Firefhip, how to prepare it.

From the bulk-head at the forecastle to a bulkhead to be raised behind the main chains, on each side and acrofs the fhip at the bulkheads, is fixed, clofe to the fhip fides, a double row of troughs, 2 feet diftance from each other, with crofs troughs quite round, at about 2 ½ feet diftance; which are mortifed into the others. The crofs troughs lead to the fides of the fhip, to the barrels and to the port-holes, to give fire both to the barrels and the chambers, to blow open the ports; and the fide-troughs ferve to communicate the fire all along the fhip and the crofs troughs.

The timbers of which the troughs are made are about 5 inches fquare; the depth of the troughs half their thicknefs, fupported by crofs pieces at every 2 or 3 yards, nailed to the timbers of the fhip, and to the wood work which inclofes the fore and main mafts, and takes in an oblong in the middle of the deck, extending to the outfide of both the mafts and in breadth is near one half of the deck; and is what makes the carpenter's room for his ftores. The decks and troughs are all well paved with mel.ed rofin.

On each fide of the fhip are cut out 6 fmall port holes, in fize about 15 by 18 inches, the ports opening downwards, are clofe caulked up: againft each port is fixed an iron chamber, which, at the time of firing the fhip, blows open the ports and lets out the fire. At the main and fore chains on each fide is a wooden funnel fixed over a fire barrel, and comes through a fcuttle in the deck up to the fhrouds to give fire to them; and between them are cut two fcuttles on each fide the fhip, which alfo ferve to let out the fire. Both funnels and fcuttles muft be ftopt with plugs, and have fail-cloth or canvas nailed clofe over them, to prevent any accident happening that way by fire to the combuftibles below.

The port-hole, funnels, and fcuttles, not only ferve to give the fire a free paffage to the outfide and upper

L 3

parts

parts of the fhip, and its rigging, but alfo for the inward air, otherwife confined, to expand itfelf, and pufh through thofe holes at the time of the combuftibles being on fire, and prevent the blowing up the decks, which otherwife muft of courfe happen from fuch a fudden and violent rarefaction of the air as will then be produced.

In the bulkhead behind on each fide is cut a fmall hole, large enough to receive a trough of the fame fize as the others; from which, to each fide of the fhip, lies a leading trough, one end coming through a fally port cut through the fhip's fide; and the other, fixing into a communicating trough that lies along the bulkhead, from one fide of the fhip to the other, and being laid with quickmatch only, at the time of firing either of the leading troughs, communicates the fire in an inftant to the contrary fide of the fhip, and both fides burn together. The communicating trough, which is fixed to the bulkhead, and the leading troughs, are the fame fize as the others.

Manner of preparing Stores.

Fire Barrels.

The form of the barrels fhould be cylindric, both upon the account of that make anfwering better for filling them with reeds, and for ftowing them on board between the troughs; their infide diameters are fufficient, if about 21 inches, and their lengths 33. The bottom parts are firft filled with fhort double-dipt reeds fet on end, and the remainder with fire-barrel compofition well mixed and melted, and then poured over them.

There are 5 holes of $\frac{1}{4}$ inch diameter, and 3 inches deep, made with a drift of that fize in the top of the compofition while it is warm; one in the centre, and the other 4 at equal diftances round the fides of the barrel. When the compofition is cold and hard, the barrel is primed by well driving thofe holes full of fuze compofition to within an inch of the top; then fixing in each

hole

hole a ftrand of quickmatch twice doubled, and in the centre hole 2 ftrands the whole length; all which muft be well fet or drove in with mealed powder; then lay the quickmatch all within the barrel, and cover the top of it with a dipt curtain, faftened on with a hoop to flip over the head, and nailed on.

The barrels fhould be made very ftrong, not only to fupport the weight of the compofition before firing, in removing and carrying them about, but to keep them together at the time they are burning; for if the ftaves are too flight and thin, and fhould burn too foon, fo as to give way, the remaining compofition would be apt to feparate, and tumble upon the deck, which would de-ftroy the defigned effect of the barrel, which is to carry the fire aloft.

Iron Chambers.

They are 10 inches long, and 3.5 in diameter; and breeched againft a piece of wood fixed acrofs the port-holes, and let into another lying a little higher; when loaded they are filled almoft full of corned powder, and have a wooden tompion well drove into their muzzles; are primed with a fmall piece of quickmatch thruft through their vents into the powder, with a part of it hanging out; and when the fhip is fired, they blow open the ports; which either fall downwards, or are carried away, and fo give vent for the fire out of the fides of the fhip.

Curtains

Are made of barras about ½ of a yard wide, and one yard in length; when they are dipped, 2 men with each a fork (on a fhaft of the fame fize, with 1 prong in each if made on purpofe) muft run each of their prongs through a corner of the curtain at the fame end; then dip them into a large kettle of compofition well melted; and when well dipped, and the curtain extended to its full breadth,

L 4　　　　　　　　whip

whip it between 2 sticks of about 5.5 feet long, and 1.5 inches square, held close by 2 other men to take off the superfluous compofition hanging to it; then immediately sprinkle saw-dust on both sides to prevent its sticking, and the curtain is finished.

N. B. A copper fixed with a furnace is much better than a kettle that is not fixed, becaufe it muft be taken off from the fire for every dipping, to prevent the stripped off compofition from falling into it, which would unavoidably give fire to the whole; and renders the ufe of a kettle tedious that way.

Reeds

Are made into fmall bundles of about 12 inches in circumference, cut even at both ends, and tied with 2 bands each; the longeft fort is 4 feet, and the fhorteft 2.5; which are all the lengths that are ufed. 1 part of them are fingle dipped, only at 1 end; the reft are double dipped, that is, at both ends. In dipping, they muft be put about 7 or 8 inches deep into a copper or kettle of melted compofition; and when drained a little over it, to carry off the fuperfluous compofition, fprinkle them over a tanned hide with pulverized fulphur, at fome diftance from the copper.

Bavins

Are made of birch, heath, or other fort of brufh-wood, that is both quickly fired and tough; in length 2.5 or 3 feet, the bufh-ends all laid one way; and the other ends tied with 2 bands each. They are dipped and fprinkled with fulphur the fame as reeds, only that the bufh-ends alone are dipped, and fhould be a little clofed together by hand as foon as done, before they are fprinkled, to keep them more clofe, to give a ftronger fire, and to keep the branches from breaking off in fhifting and handling them.

Difpofition

Difpofition of the Stores on board, when laid for firing.

The fire-barrels are placed under the funnels and fcut-tles, 1 to each; and are fixed between the crofs troughs leading to the fides of the fhip, and lafhed to them, and well cleeted to the deck. Thofe at the funnels give fire to the main and fore fhrouds; the reft rife over the deck through the fcuttles. The plugs muft be taken out of the funnels and fcuttles before the fhip is fired, and the curtains covering the fire-barrels cut open and rolled back, the quickmatch fpread, and the top of the barrels well falted with priming compofition. The curtains are nailed to the beams of the upper deck, hanging down over the troughs, bavins, and reeds.

The priming compofition; a part of it is laid along the troughs, and the reft, after laying of the reeds and bavins, is regularly ftrewed over all. The fhort reeds double dipped, with fome of the fingle dipped, are laid along both the fides and crofs troughs, and communicate the fire both to the barrels and chambers. The reft of the fingle dipped reeds and bavins are fet about the fire barrels, and to the fides of the fhip; and fome flung upon the deck.

The quickmatch is laid 2 or 3 ftrands thick upon the reeds in the troughs, and about the fire-barrels and chambers, to communicate a general fire at once. The reeds in the troughs with the quickmatch are lafhed on, to prevent their falling out by the rolling of the fhip.

The leading troughs are both laid with 4 or 5 ftrands of quickmatch; as is likewife the communicating trough, that by firing either of the leading troughs, the communicating trough may carry the fire to the other fide of the fhip; which then runs along the troughs by the quickmatch on both fides, and gives fire to the whole in an inftant.

The

The Compofition made ufe of for Curtains, Reeds, and Bavins, are all the fame, viz.

Pitch	14	
Sulphur	7	N. B. For want of tar take 3 lb. of
Rofin	7	tallow.
Tallow	2	
Tar	1	

Fire-Barrel Compofition for one Barrel.

Corned powder	lb. 120
Pitch	60
Tallow	10

Divide the compofition into 5 pots; the pitch and tallow muft be firft thoroughly melted. Tallow well the outfide of the pot to take off the heat; and then put in the powder by fmall quantities, ftirring it well about.

Priming Compofition for one Barrel.

Corn powder	lb. 100
Petre	50
Sulphur	40
Rofin	6
Oil	pints 3

Take 20 lb. of powder, which mix well with the petre, fulphur, and rofin; work them well together, breaking it well in working; then put the reft of the powder in by degrees, and work it all together: fpread it in a trough, and through a hair fieve run 3 pints of oil all over it: then work it well together, and run it through a cane fieve.

N. B.

N. B. In the following eſtimate for the quantity of ſtores requiſite, the reeds for the barrels are not included; it will take 100 ſhort double dipped more than theſe ſpecified; but their value is included in the article of barrels.

Stores for a Fireſhip of 150 Tons.

	Numb.	Value.
		l. : *s.* : *d.*
Fire barrels	8	80 : 0 : 0
Iron chambers	12	12 : 0 : 0
Priming compoſition barrels	3½	21 : 0 : 0
Quickmatch barrels	1	3 : 0 : 0
Curtains dipped	30	3 : 0 : 0
Long reeds ſingle dipped	150	10 : 15 : 0
Short reeds { double dipped	75	2 : 18 : 9
{ ſingle dipped	75	1 : 17 : 6
Bavins ſingle dipped	209	10 : 0 : 0
		144 : 11 : 3

Quantity of Compoſition for preparing the Stores of a Fireſhip.

	pe-tre.	ſulp	corn pow.	pit ch	ro-ſin	tal low	tar	oil pts.
For 8 barrels	0	0	960	480	0	80	0	0
For 3. 5 barrels of priming compoſition	175	140	350	0	21	0	0	11
For the curtains, bavins, and reeds for the ſhip, and ſulphur for ſalting them	0	200	0	350	175	50	25	0
Total	175	340	1310	830	196	130	25	1 1

Total weight of the compoſition 3017, equal to C. 28 : 3 : 2.

Compoſition

Compofition allowed for the reeds for the barrels one fifth of the whole of the laft article, which is equal to 163 lb. and makes the whole 3177 pounds, or C. 28 : 1 : 13.

We have completed the feveral branches of the Art of War, in eight volumes in octavo, as promifed. We have done all that lies in our power to treat them with perfpi-cuity and clearnefs, in order to reduce the whole to as fmall a compafs as poffible, for the fake of thofe military gentlemen who have an inclination to be mafters of their bufinefs in a fhort time. We could not enlarge upon every particular fo much as might be neceffary; yet who-ever renders himfelf mafter of what we have faid, will find that nothing very material has been neglected.

BELIDOR

M. BELIDOR's New Method of MINING.

To which is added,

M. VALLIERE on COUNTERMINES.

THIS work is, to shew the fallacy of miners in general, in regard to the effect of powder confined in mines, and to establish the true theory of mines, upon a solid foundation; which being likewise confirmed by many unexceptionable experiments, cannot fail of meeting with the approbation of every unprejudiced reader: as to those who find fault with every thing new, that seems to contradict an old established opinion, though ever so erroneous, their censures will not be regarded; nor will any objection whatever be admitted, unless supported by well attested experiments.

If you imagine a large globe of earth homogeneous in all its parts, and a certain quantity of powder lodged in its centre, so as to produce a proper effect without bursting the globe; by setting fire to the powder, it is evident, that the explosion will act all round, to overcome the obstacles which oppose its motion; and as the particles of earth are porous, they will compress each other in proportion as the flame increases, and the capacity of the chamber increases likewise. But the particles of earth next to the chamber will communicate a part of their motion to those next to them, and those to their neighbours; and this communication will thus continue in a decreasing proportion, till the whole force of explosion is entirely spent, and the particles of earth beyond this term will remain in the same state as they were. The

particles

particles of earth that have been acted upon by the force of explosion will compose a globe which M. Belidor calls the *Globe of Compression.*

The foregoing experiment is easily comprehended; but when powder is lodged in a mine, where the weight of the earth in the line of least resistance, is less than at the sides and underneath, it seemingly appears, that as soon as the force of explosion reaches the surface of the ground, it would throw up a certain quantity of earth, and leave a hollow in the form of a frustum of a cone, with no other effect upon the sides or bottom; as likewise, that when the mine is overcharged, the base of the excavation, instead of increasing, would rather diminish, because the force of explosion being greater would sooner reach the extremity of the line of least resistance: it is in this light, that all practical miners have hitherto considered the action of powder lodged in mines; and from thence concluded, that a certain charge will form an excavation, whose greatest diameter shall be double the line of least resistance; a less quantity raise the earth only a little, and a greater throw the earth up higher, and diminish the diameter of the excavation instead of increasing it.

As absurd as such an opinion may be, that a greater force produces a less effect than a more moderate one; yet it has prevailed amongst all the practical miners in Europe; without considering that there may be physical causes in nature, with which they were unacquainted, and that no theory of this kind should be admitted unless supported by well attested experiments.

M. Belidor made several experiments with various charges at la Fere, from which it appeared, that the greatest diameter of an excavation may not only be made double, but treble or quadruple; yet some old miners of note, who were present, could or would not believe it, though they had seen it, much less those who were absent. These experiments shewed that the diameter of the excavation could be made greater than was imagined; but for what reason, was not hitherto known, till M. Belidor demonstrated it, in the Memoirs of the Academy of Sciences

ences at Paris, in 1762, from which this work has been extracted.

To explain the reasons on which the principles of mines are grounded, it is necessary to consider not only the resistance which the weight of the earth and the cohesion of the parts make against the force of explosion, but likewise the pression of the atmosphere, which is so great as to counterbalance a column of water of the same base, and whose altitude is 33 feet, which answers nearly to a height of a middling soil of about 22 feet: so that if the line of least resistance of a mine is 10 feet, the force of explosion must not only overcome the weight of 10 feet of earth above it, but 32 feet, properly speaking. It is to be observed, that this weight resists the force of explosion no longer than till the mine bursts, and the explosion gets a communication with the air, because then the pressure of the air ceases.

Plate I. fig. 1. As the powder does not fire all at once, but gradually; so the force of explosion increases proportionally, and condenses the earth all round in a spheric form, as has been observed, till this force overcomes the resistance of the earth and atmosphere, which cannot happen before the earth rises in the middle into a spheric form, and the radius (C A) of explosion extends to the surface (A B) of the earth; and then the explosion getting a free communication with the air, raises the earth to a considerable height, and forms an excavation of a curve-lined figure, such as A E B; the point C represents the centre of the powder or chamber.

It is a known principle, established by facts, that the force of explosion is always proportional to the quantity of powder fired; and as the force of explosion acts in a spheric form, and spheres are as the cubes of their radii, it is evident, that the forces of explosion, or the quantities of powder fired, are proportional to the cubes of their radii.

This proportion will always hold good in an uniform soil but varies according to the density: and if the chamber of a mine be placed on a rock, or some other hard substance, the diameter of the excavation will be greater

than

than it would have been otherwise; becaufe the force of
explofion being refifted downwards, will act with a greater
violence towards the fides and upwards. A mine placed
in a foil of a greater denfity and tenacity than another of
the fame depth, requires a greater charge in proportion;
but it muft be obferved, that the tenacity is not proportional to the furface of the excavation, as M. de Valliere,
and fome others pretend, but to the folid itfelf, as we
have fhewn in page 221 of our Attack, where we treat
of the proper charges of mines.

To find a proper charge of a mine in any foil, fo as to
produce a given diameter, an experiment mine muft be
made in the fame foil, fufficiently charged, fo as to produce
a proper effect, and the line of leaft refiftance exactly mea-
fured, as well as the diameter of the opening, by which
the radius C A of the globe of compreffion will be found:
then fay, *the cube of the radius of the globe of compreffion
found by the experiment, is to the cube of the radius of the
propofed mine, as the charge of the experiment mine is to the
charge required.*

And to find the diameter of a mine whofe charge is
given, fay, *the charge of the experiment mine is to the given
charge, as the cube of the radius of the firft is to the cube of
the radius of the fecond.* From whence the diameter required is found by this equation, $CA^2 - CD^2 = AD^2$

Amongft fome mines made at la Fere, one was charged
with 170lb. and another with 300lb. the line of leaft
refiftance of both was 10 feet: the diameters being mea-
fured, the firft was found 20 feet, and the fecond 27.
Now to find this laft diameter by the theory, add the
fquares of 10, the line of leaft refiftance, to the fquare
of 10, half the diameter 20, which gives 200, for the
fquare of the radius whofe cube is 2828: then 170 :
300 : : 2828 : 4990, this fourth term is the cube of the
radius of the fecond mine, whofe root is 17: and if
from the fquare 289 of this root, the fquare 100 of the
line of leaft refiftance be fubtracted, the fquare root of
the difference will be 13.7 and 27.4, twice this root, the
                                                    diameter

diameter required: which is nearly the same as has been found by the experiment.

Let a mine be loaded with 980lb. in the same soil, and the line of least resistance 15 feet: then 170 : 980 : : 2828 : 16302 : for the cube of the radius, and its logarithm 4.21224, multiplied by 2, and divided by 3, gives 2.80826; for the logarithm of the square of the radius, which answers to the number 643, from which subtracting 225, the square of the line of least resistance, and taking the square root of the difference 418, we get 20.4, and twice that number gives 40.8, which exceeds 40 feet 2 inches, found by experiment, by about 5 inches.

Having made another mine in the same soil, loaded with 3600lb. of powder, and of the same depth, viz. 15 feet, the diameter was found to be 70 feet: now if 170 : 3600 : : 2828 : 59887, this fourth term is the cube of the radius, whose logarithm, 4.77733, multiplied by 2 and divided by 3, gives 3.184888 for the logarithm of the square, which therefore is 1530; from this subtracting 225, the square of the line of least resistance, the square root of the difference 1305 will be 36, and twice this number 72 the diameter; which is 2 feet more than that found by experiment.

M. Belidor, finding the diameters of mines loaded with great charges, greater by computation than by experiments, imagines that it was owing to the cubical chambers, by which the quantity of earth above them is less in proportion than in small ones: but whether this reason is just, or that the diameter and the line of least resistance have not been rightly measured, is not certain; for a friend of mine found the contrary in some very accurate experiments he made.

Having given an account in page 232 of our Attack, of some experiments formerly made at la Fere, and computed their diameters from the parabolic figure, we shall here compute the same diameters from the globe of compression. The first was loaded with 120, the second 160, the third 200, the fourth 240, the fifth 280, the sixth 320, and the seventh with 360: the line of least resistance was

10 feet in all of them; the diameters were found to be, 1ft, 22 ⅔, 2d, 26, 3d, 29, 4th, 31¼, 5th, 33½, 6th, 36, 7th, 38 feet. Now taking the diameter of any one as known, for example, that of the second 26, whose globe of compreſſion will be found to be 4412; then as the globes of compreſſion are proportional to the charges, they will be, 1ft, 3309; 3d, 5515; 4th, 6618; 5th, 7721; 6th, 8824; 7th, 9927: the ſquares of their radii, 1ft, 225.05; 3d, 312.15; 4th, 352.49; 5th, 390.64; 6th, 427.02; 7th, 461.9; and the radii of the baſes, 1ft, 11.05; 3d, 14.56; 4th, 15.88; 5th, 17.04; 6th, 18.08; 7th, 19.02; whence the diameters are, 22.1; 29.12; 31.76; 34.08; 36.16; 38; which ſhews that the greateſt difference between the meaſured and computed diameters is not above 6 inches.

The near agreement between the diameters, computed from theſe two different methods, ſeemingly ſo different, appears extraordinary. I found beſides, in computing large tables by both of them, that one gave the charge ſomething greater than equal, and afterwards leſs than the other; but the differences were immaterial.

We have hitherto computed the diameters of mines from their charges; we ſhall now give ſome examples to ſhew how to find the charges, from the given diameters. Thus a mine made in the ſame ſoil as the laſt ſeven, whoſe line of leaſt reſiſtance is 10 feet, it is required to find the charge ſo as to make a diameter of 40 feet: the ſum of the ſquares of the line of leaſt reſiſtance 10, and half the diameter 20, gives 500 for the ſquare of the radius of the globe of compreſſion; and the ſquare root 22.36 of 500, multiplied by 500, gives 11180 for the globe of compreſſion; then the globe of compreſſion 4412 of the ſecond mine, is to the globe of compreſſion 11180, as the charge 160 of the experiment mine is to the charge required, which will be 405lb. nearly.

Let a mine whoſe line of leaſt reſiſtance is 10 feet be loaded with 170lb. of powder, and have a diameter of 20 feet; it is propoſed to make another in the ſame ſoil, whoſe line of leaſt reſiſtance is 15 feet, and its diameter

70, to find its charge. The square 1225 of half the diameter 70, added to the square 225 of the line of leaft refiftance 10, gives 1450, whofe root is 38 nearly; and 1450, multiplied by 38, gives 55100 for the globe of compreffion, and as the globe of compreffion of the experiment mine has been found above to be 2828, we have 2828 : 55100 :: 170 : 3312lb. of powder for the charge required.

M. Belidor fays, to fhew the application of the globe of compreffion in the defence of places, I fhall explain the planes and profils of countermines made at la Fere, to blow up the befiegers cannons, and throw them into the ditch, together with another experiment, which threw the cannons into the fortification.

It is well known, that when once the befiegers have eftablifhed their batteries near the covered way, to make a breach in an outwork, or the body of the place, they become practicable in 2 or 3 days, then the befieged are obliged to furrender; fo that the only refource remaining to them, is to retard the finifhing thefe batteries as much as poffible, by all the ftratagems that can be imagined; but nothing difconcerts the befiegers fo much as the deftroying them by countermines, and to throw the cannons into the poffeffion of the befieged.

Every time that batteries have been deftroyed by countermines, the cannons have been thrown into the trenches, becaufe the refiftance is greater on the fide of the parapet than on any other; but when the fame ground is blown up feveral times, the chambers may be fo difpofed, that when the befiegers have re-eftablifhed their batteries for the fecond or third time, the cannons may be blown towards the place; becaufe the earth to fill up the excavation having much lefs tenacity than the former, that fide which was the ftrongeft becomes the weakeft.

By following this method, I have in 1724 conftructed countermines under the glacis of the polygon at la Fere, to blow up the batteries fuppofed to be erected by the befiegers three times.

M 2   Plate

Plate I. Fig. 2, 3, 4. The firft chamber C, blew up two 24 pounders towards the trenches as ufual : the batteries being re-eftablifhed, the chamber D threw the cannons into the ditch : the batteries being re-eftablifhed again, the chamber E threw the cannons again into the ditch, to the great furprife of the fpeftators, efpecially to fome of the miners, who expected quite the contrary. For it was the firft time that this method had been practifed except at the fiege of Turin in 1706, where by chance one of our pieces was thrown into the covert-way, which the befieged carried in triumph into the town.

As fuch an advantage is extremely proper to raife the courage of the garrifon, and to difcourage the befiegers, by the length of time to re-eftablifh the batteries, we thought we could not fhew better our attachment to his majefty's fervice, than endeavouring to improve this branch of the countermines, in fuch a manner, that the firft mine, called fougafle, having only eight or ten feet of the line of the leaft refiftance, may throw directly the enemy's guns into the ditch of the place, and even into the work, in order to make ufe of them againft him. This method may be ufed in places which have wet ditches as well as the dry; fince by finking only 3 feet under the level of the covert way, the height of the banquet and parapet give 7 feet more, this makes a fufficient line of leaft refiftance to blow up a battery. If 8 feet can be funk inftead of 3, the battery may be twice blown up, and a third time if 13 or 14 feet can be funk. The queftion is then to throw the cannons the firft time into the ditch; for after that, there is no doubt but it may be done again as often as the enemy attempts to raife them, and the depth of the ground will allow it.

This project being fent to court, was ordered to be put in practice in 1739 ; for which reafon a battery was raifed in all its forms, for two 24 pounders. Under the middle of which a gallery F G, fig. 5, 6, was made from the foot T, of the banquet of 20 feet long, from which 2 branches GH, GI, were made, each of them 7 feet long, to place the chambers A A, whofe lines of

leaft

leaft refiftance was 7 feet only, being under the axle-trees
of the pieces; the gallery was continued in a flope, to
make from thence 2 other branches K L, K N, in the
fame manner as the preceding, but lower, to place
the chambers B, B, whofe line of leaft refiftance was
10 feet, and at the fame diftance from the former A,
taken horizontally, in order to have the right angled
ifofecles triangle B D C, fig. 5, whofe hypothenufe B C,
fhews the direction of the action of the powder.

The intent of the little chambers A, A, being to overcome the tenacity of the foil, without any other effect,
were charged each with 20 pounds of powder only, whereas the others B, B, were each charged with 600 pounds.
The length of the leaders were contrived fo as the fire
being fet to it at F, it went to G, and from thence to
the chambers A, A, and to the point K at the fame time,
and to the chambers B, B, in a few feconds afterwards:
the firft, A, A. having produced a proper effect, the
fecond B, B, met with lefs refiftance towards the wheels
of the carriages than towards the trail, raifed the pieces
to about 40 fathoms, and then threw them 35 fathoms
from the battery into the ditch.

The effect of thefe mines was much greater than expected, even by thofe who had the moft favourable opi-
nions, from the bare expofition of the project: the moft
expert in mines at la Fere were more fenfible than ever of
the certainty of the principles eftablifhed in our theory,
and of all the advantages that may be obtained from the
globe of compreffion.

Though the centres of the two chambers were 18 feet
from each other, they yet produced but one excavation
of an elliptic form, whofe greateft diameter was found
to be 45 feet, and the leaft 27; the depth 18, and the
bottom well cleared, without hurting the parapet of the
covert way. If then 2 mines produced fo great an excavation, to what extremity will the befiegers be reduced
if a battery of 10 or 12 pieces was blown up: for where
will they find earth enough to fill up an excavation of 35
or 40 fathoms in length, 5 in breadth, and 15 feet deep?

M 3   What

What time will be loft in repairing all thefe damages; and what deftruction there muft be amongft the foldiers, from the fire of fhells, carcaffes, and granades, continually thrown into fuch a confined place!

Experiments made at BISY in July, 1753, by order of the French King, together with their Ufe in the Attack of Places.

THE intent of thefe experiments was to render ufelefs the countermines of a befieged town, by burfting the galleries all round, above and below, to a certain diftance, or to change thefe galleries into fo many trenches, by which the covert-way may be taken at once with very little trouble. His majefty being informed of thefe means, ordered that experiments fhould be made near the caftle of Bify, belonging to the duke of Belleifle. In confequence of which, a detachment of 75 miners, with their officers, was fent there from the artillery fchool at la Fere. The work begun with what belongs to the globe of compreffion; a foil had been pitched upon the moft uniform that could be found, which happened to be a hard fand, mixed with gravel; there were made 4 galleries, A, B, C, D, fig. 7, 3 feet wide, and 6 high, fo as to form a rectangle, whofe fides anfwered nearly to the 4 cardinal points : the 2 oppofite ones A, B, which faced the north and fouth, were each 10 fathoms long, and the other 2 C, D, which faced the weft and eaft, 12 fathoms; they were lined with ftones, in order to fhew that mafonry was rather an advantage than an obftacle to the effect of powder: the bottom of thefe galleries had a flope of 6 feet 3 inches, and the mean depth was 15 feet under the furface of the ground, which terminated in a defcent from fouth to north, between the interval of the galleries of that name. In that to the eaft, C, a branch, L K, was made at right angles of 24 feet long, and at K another, K F, at right angle to this, to place a chamber, E, 30 feet diftant from the gallery A, 36 from D, and 42 from

B.

B. The other galleries were made by means of 2 shafts or pits, M, I, the one M, to the south was 16 feet deep, and the other, I, to the north 20.

When these galleries were finished, the last pit, I, was deepened nine feet more; so that the bottom Y, fig. 8, was 29 feet below the surface of the ground near the chamber. After this a gallery, YX, was made going directly under the chamber E, with a descent of 18 inches, and 5 feet high, by which its top was 14 feet below the centre of the chamber E, the whole supported with strong planks of oak, and still in the same sort of soil as mentioned before, but so hard, that the miners were obliged to use the chiffels. Such was the disposition made to what belonged to the globe of compreffion; whose object was to see whether it would burst all these galleries.

As it does not appear natural, that a mine, whose effect should be on the weakest side, would burst galleries at a distance of 4 times the length of its line of least resistance, it is no wonder that it should have been doubted; though the experiment made at la Fere in 1732, should have been a proof of it, as the fact was established upon the preceding theory, yet the miners were not convinced, pretending that the powder had penetrated between the soft soil and a bed of strong clay, so far as to burst the gallery. It was plain, that by admitting this theory, the old, and all its consequences, must of necessity be rejected. I kept silence upon this article till 1753, when, in a discourse which I had the honour to make to his majesty on the effect of powder in mines and fire-arms, he ordered immediately that I should be furnished with means to make farther experiments, which are those I have now described.

The 18th of June, the count d'Argenson, who arrived the night before at the duke of Belleifle's, at the castle of Bify, with some general officers and other persons of quality, who came there out of curiosity, went early in the morning, to visit all the works of the mines; after this fire was set to the globe of compreffion, which

has

had been loaded the night before with 3000 lb. of powder : it raifed the earth to about 150 feet high. They
then went to fee whether it had deftroyed the galleries
about it, as well as thofe underneath, and to what diftance the globe of compreffion had acted; it was found
that it formed an excavation perfectly round of 66 feet
diameter, and 17 deep.

The eaft gallery C, lined with mafonry, and at 24
feet diftant from the chamber, was entirely burft from
one end to the other.

The fouth gallery A, at 30 feet diftant from the
chamber, was equally burft from one end to the other,
except 2 fathoms near the entrance M, at the weft.

The weft gallery D, of 12 fathoms long, and 36 feet
diftant from the chamber, was deftroyed to the length of
7 fathoms, 3 fathoms were left near its entrance at the
north, and 2 fathoms on the other end.

The north gallery B, which was 10 fathoms long,
and 42 feet from the chamber, was deftroyed all but
2 fathoms at its entrance at the weft, fo there was 8 fathoms impracticable, which were divided into 2 equal
parts by the perpendicular drawn from the centre of the
chamber to that gallery.

As that line formed a right-angled triangle, with half
the gallery deftroyed, whofe hypothenufe is 48 feet;
which hypothenufe is the radius of the globe of compreffion; this fhews that the globe of compreffion would
have deftroyed a gallery at that diftance, and confequently
quadruple the line of leaft refiftance.

The gallery Y, Z, S, fig. 8, which paffed under the
chamber E, whofe top was 14 feet from it, and length
69 feet, could not be entered farther than the length
Y Z of 24½ feet, fo that 45 feet of it was deftroyed;
as the extremity of this gallery was 9 feet beyond the
centre of the chamber, it appears that there remains
60 feet from the middle to the entrance, and as there
were 24 feet not deftroyed, there remained 36 deftroyed
on that fide, which taking for the bafe of a right-angled
triangle Z S E, and the perpendicular E S being 14 feet,
the

the hypothenuse E Z, is found to be 38 feet, which therefore is the radius of the globe of compreffion: fo that it would have deftroyed a gallery whofe top had been at that diftance under the mine, confequently 50 feet under the furface of the ground, which is the greateft diftance that a gallery can ever be made. Thefe are facts yet extant, and which may be verified upon the fpot.

From hence it follows, that if the line of leaft refiftance had been 15 or 16 feet inftead of 12, the globe of compreffion would have deftroyed a gallery at 60 feet diftant from the centre of the chamber; confequently if the chamber was placed at that depth, and nearly in the middle between two liftning galleries, whofe diftance is generally from 15 to 24 fathoms, it would have burfted both the envelope and all thofe under and above them, by increafing only the quantity of powder in proportion. This proves the great ufe that may be made of the globe of compreffion, in the attack of a place countermined.

It has been found, that to make ufe of the globe of compreffion in a common foil, the chamber fhould be made upon the fame level with the galleries, and its greateft diftance be about quadruple its depth nearly; then the diameter of the excavation will be about fextuple that line. And to find the charge, *multiply 3 times the line of leaft refiftance, expreffed in feet by 100, and the product will give the number of pounds of powder for the charge required.* For example, having 2 or 3 contiguous galleries, 15 feet deep, at a diftance not exceeding 60 feet; make a fhaft in the moft convenient place, and from thence carry a branch to eftablifh the chamber: then 3 times 15, the depth of the mine, multiplied by 100, gives 4500 lb. for the charge of this mine. From this rule it appears, that the true charge of the globe of compreffion at Bify fhould have been 3600 lb. for a line of leaft refiftance of 12 feet, then the diameter of the excavation would have been 72 feet inftead of 66, and in that cafe the weft gallery would have been deftroyed to the

the quadruple of the line of leaſt reſiſtance, as already mentioned. The reaſon for charging the mine of Biſy with 3000 lb. only, was to prevent ſome houſes near it, from being damaged. This rule for charging mines is not founded on any exact theory, but is ſufficiently exact, becauſe it is better in this caſe, to make the charge greater than leſs.

While part of the miners detachment was occupied in what belonged to the globe of compreſſion, the other was at work to conſtruct a place of arms of a covert-way to countermine it; in order to change them afterwards into trenches of a ſiege, and to furniſh means of a new kind of experiments. This place of arms traced ſuch as one in a real fortification was found to be in a moſt un-grateful ſoil, for the bottom was of a very hard free ſtone, that could not be penetrated without blowing it up; and it was covered with a ſtrong clay, which ap-peared to be againſt the intended experiments ; but as it would have been looked upon to favour the experiments, by changing the ſituation, it was thought proper to con-tinue the work in that ſoil which had been pitched upon by chance, ſo that if they ſucceeded in this, there would be no doubt of their ſucceſs in any other.

Plate II. Fig. 12. At the depth of 12, 13, 14, and 15 feet, were made a gallery *magiſtrate* 1, 2, 3; an *envelope* 4 7, at the foot of the glacis; 2 traverſing, 1, 4 and 3, 7; and 2 *liſtner*, 5, 8 and 6, 9; all being 5 feet high, and 3 broad. This work being finiſhed, a ſap, B C, was made in the uſual form, which croſſing one of the liſtners, and within about 4 fathoms of the other, as happened by chance. The 16th, the beſieged miners intending to deſtroy this head of the ſap, ſet fire to the mines A, B, carried from the liſtner at the right. The ſecond mine B, which was 10 feet deep, formed an excavation of 27 feet diameter, in which the miners entered to diſcover the gallery, cleared it, and from thence entered into the liſtner, which was done in 5 hours.

T   T

The 11th, the besiegers intending to destroy, at the same time, and by the same fire, the listner of 20 fathoms, the envelope of 24, and 12 of the traversing; in order to which, they begun at the right to place sand bags before them serving as a retrenchment, then placed the leaders and put ten barrels of powder in two heaps at the end of the traversing gallery; 16 in 4 heaps into the envelope, and as much into the listner; and stopped up the entrance at the excavation: all this work was finished in 7 hours.

The count d'Argenson being arrived, the besieged miners set fire to the mine C, at the left, which they had loaded with 200 lb. of powder, in order to destroy the sap on that side. The besiegers miners entered into the excavation, to discover the gallery; in the mean time the besieged sent 2 miners, followed by lord Melford, out of curiosity, to observe the besiegers, who being arrived at the envelope, the smoke of the leader was so great, that they could proceed no further; then retired in haste into the fresh air, to recover from the suffocation they were affected with in the attempt.

An hour after, the same lord, with a serjeant and a corporal, entered a second time into the gallery, to see whether they could advance farther, but found the stench of the powder still worse than the first time; for attempting to go into the listner, they swooned away, and would have died, had they not been carried out directly, especially the corporal, who did not recover in 24 hours. This example shews, that the miners have not a more cruel enemy than the confined smoke of powder; for if they are in it during a few minutes, faint away, and die if not properly secured.

After this event, fire was set to the leader on the right, which suddenly raised the upper part of the listner, the envelope and part of the traversing, and changed them into trenches, as in fig 13. to the length of 56 fathoms, being about 24 feet broad, and about 8 deep; a little after

after were fprung by the fame fire, the reft of the communication or traverfing adjacent, with half the magiftral in the gorge of the place of arms, by means of 24
barrels of powder placed in fix heaps, which changed
thefe galleries alfo into trenches, the length of 38 fathoms,
that is, the liftner on the right, the envelope, the
traverfing, and the magiftral, formed one continued
trench.

The fame day the miners, after having cleared the
bottom of the excavation near the liftner at the left,
opened the gallery and penetrated into the liftner, charged it and the traverfing with 20 barrels of powder
placed in 4 heaps; they charged likewife the other half
of the magiftral gallery, in the place of arms, with 12
barrels of powder placed in 3 heaps.

Things thus difpofed, the count d'Argenfon and the
duke of Belleifle came the 19th, to fee the remainder of
the operations; the firft changed the liftner, which was
22 fathoms long, into a trench with more fuccefs than
the former, as being better cleared; after this, the reft
of the magiftral gallery was fprung, which made a
trench of 20 fathoms. Thefe trenches may be traverfed
and finifhed, as in fig. 11.

It may perhaps be faid, that as thefe countermines
were not defended, it is no wonder that thefe trenches
were fo eafily made: but this objection deferves no
anfwer; it is fufficient, that the operations made here
are what is daily practifed at the fchool of artillery,
without any body receiving the leaft harm.

All thefe experiments being finifhed to the fatisfaction
of the count d'Argenfon, without any accident, that mi-
nifter, to verify them to the king, had a memorial drawn
up, and figned by Meffrs. Valiere, Gourdon, lieutenant
generals; d'Auville, Chateaufer, Gribauval, captains
of miners; Belcourt, third commander of the fchool of
artillery at la Fere and Belidor.

It is after this memorial that the preceding facts have
been written, which cannot be fufpected of any altera-
tions,

tions, every thing was approved of by all who were invited by M. Count d'Argenſon, to ſee them.

From theſe experiments has been deduced a method for changing galleries of mines into trenches, viz. after having ſtopt the entrance with ſand bags or wood, the heaps of barrels of powder ſhould be placed at equal diſtances from each other, to make them take fire together, and this diſtance ſhould not exceed triple the depth of the gallery, from thence the length of the leaders will be determined. The charge ſhould not be too great, to prevent the making too deep a trench, for the ſoldiers to defend them; each heap of powder ſhould contain as many barrels of 100 lb. as there are feet in the fourth part of the depth of the gallery, in a common ſoil. For example, having a gallery of about 24 fathoms, and 16 feet deep, there ſhould be 4 barrels in a heap, and 4 heaps, diſtant 6 fathoms from the centre of the one to the centre of the next, and half that diſtance from the ends. This may be done in 4 hours. If the galleries were ſituated in a different ſoil, than that we have here ſuppoſed, a trial muſt be made to determine from thence the proper charge.

To account for the effect of powder in galleries of mines changed into trenches; I conſider that theſe galleries are in the ſame caſe as a muſket that is to be burſt, which requires not to be charged with a great quantity of powder. For if its end be well ſtopped, when the powder is fired, the flame being prevented from ruſhing out, endeavours to extend itſelf, till a ſufficient quantity is fired to overcome the obſtacle that reſiſts it, opens the barrel from one end to the other. The ſame thing happens in galleries of mines; for when the heaps of powder are properly diſpoſed, and the leaders ſo contrived as the ſeveral heaps take fire at the ſame time, the flame extends all over till a ſufficient quantity is lighted to burſt the gallery. From hence it follows,

1. That the method of changing galleries of mines into trenches, will be of excellent uſe, eſpecially when the ſoil is gravel or ſtony, which is improper to proceed

ceed by fap; for this is no hindrance to the effect of powder, as found by the experiments made at Bily.

2. That the countermines, as commonly made in a fortified place, are a difadvantage to the befieged inftead of an advantage; efpecially, if the befiegers have plans and profils of them, becaufe they cannot fpring an advanced mine, without giving the enemy an opportunity to burft their galleries, and advance to the covert-way with very little trouble, and to erect batteries with fecurity.

3. Henceforward, the chance of the befieged and befiegers will entirely be changed, fince the latter will find difpofitions ready prepared, which will turn more to his advantage, than the place could formerly have received from them.

4. That in the attack of places countermined, the befiegers miners will be of much greater importance than ever; fince the taking the covert-way will be their lot, as well as all thofe works which have under-ground communications with the place, fuch as the citadel of Tournay and many others, and the place itfelf, if it has any fuch paffages.

5. That the prefent method of making countermines, leading towards the covert-way, muft neceffarily be changed, in order to prevent the enemy from turning the galleries to his advantage.

Plate III. Fig. 17. To apply our method of attacking the countermines in a place befieged, I fuppofed, the firft and fecond parallels made the latter A, B, C, to be di-ftant of about 60 fathoms from the pallifades of the covert-way, and from thence the trenches are carried on in the capital of the ravelin, and in thofe of the adjacent baftions of the front attacked; and after this, batteries I, are made of cannons and mortars to enfilade by rico-chet, the covert-way, and the ramparts parallel to it, to deftroy their defences. During this time, the fapers carry on the faps towards the places of arms in the co-vert way, both faliant and rentring; to eftablifh the heads E F near the ends of the liftners G, G, before
the

the faliant angles, and the miners proceed under-ground to place chambers I, overcharged, between the extremities of the liftners of the re-entring angles : I fuppofe they have taken the precaution to fink their fhafts as deep as the countermines, that the chambers may nearly be upon a level with the galleries, and that the fhafts are placed in the trenches K, which lead from one battery to the other, not to interfere with any other works; from the bottom of thefe fhafts they make the galleries K L of about 20 fathoms long. This will be a work of 4 or 5 days to the eftablifhing their chambers, which fhould be finifhed at the fame time, that they may be fprung together ; the fapers will by this time be arrived to the heads E F, to induce the befieged to fpring fome of their mines, to deftroy them ; with a little attention his intention may be difcovered time enough to withdraw the troops.

Suppofing, that they have fprung 2 or 3 mines at each fide, as foon as this is done, the miners enter into the excavations to difcover the galleries, which they muft do at the fame time, while the fapers form a lodgment in the excavation. When the galleries are found and cleared, they ftop up their entrances, to keep in the fmoke till they want to make ufe of them. On the other hand, all the globes of compreffion are fired, and from their excavations fearch is made on the right and left to difcover the liftners ; fo that, if the meafures have been rightly taken, 14 entrances into the countermines will be found, by which it will be out of the befieged's power to refift equally every where ; fhould there be but half that number practicable, it would be fufficient to get poffeffion of all their mines; of which, only thofe that are convenient to advance the fiege, are to be changed into trenches.

Obfervations on the preceding Theory.

That this theory grounded on the globe of compreffion, is a great improvement upon the art of mining,

muft

muſt be allowed: the experiments made at Bify and la Fere, before many military gentlemen, demonſtrate its great effects, and intirely overſet that old erroneous opinion, hitherto believed by miners in general, that powder confined in mines acts on the weakeſt ſide, and not downwards nor ſide-ways. Since galleries were deſtroyed under and at the ſides of the chamber, at the diſtance equal to four times the line of leaſt reſiſt-ance; whereas before it was ſuppoſed that it could not make the diameter of the excavation above twice that line. Therefore, as long as this erroneous opinion, in-ſiſted upon by all authors, ſubſiſted, the theory of mines could not be brought to any degree of perfection.

The method of throwing the cannons of batteries placed on the covert-way, into the ditch, is no leſs important, ſince nothing can diſhearten the beſiegers ſo much, as to ſee their batteries for making a breach deſtroyed as oft as they attempt to raiſe or repair them. It may be obſer-ved that the ſmall mines A, Plate I. fig. 6. ſeem not to be abſolutely neceſſary, provided the great ones B, are placed directly under the breech of the gun; for in this caſe, as the part of the gun and carriage towards the place is much heavier than the other, if the mine be properly charged, muſt throw the guns towards the ditch, with-out the help of theſe ſmall mines; for this has been effected by one mine only, at Byfleet camp, ſome years ago, by Matthew Clark, one of the greateſt engineers of his time.

The greateſt advantage of this theory conſiſts in changing the galleries of countermines into trenches of an attack; ſince it reduces the moſt dangerous and dif-ficult part of a ſiege, which is that from the third paral-lel to the intire poſſeſſion of the covert-way, into a very ſhort and ſafe method, ſuppoſing the place counter-mined. This method is however liable to ſome ob-jections; M. Belidor mentions one; which is, *that it may be ſaid, the countermines in the place of arms not having been defended, it is not to be wondered that ſuch an advan-tage has been made of them:* without any other anſwer than
what

what is daily practised at la Fere. Now if the besieged
are prevented by the smoke to enter into the galleries, does not the same difficulty obstruct the besiegers?
It is true, he says afterwards, that the entrance from the
excavation is kept stopped till they want to use them,
and when opened, the air enters at one end and drives
out the smoke through the other. But then so soon as
the gallery is cleared from the smoke, it may be entered at
both ends, by which the besieged can with an equal advantage defend them, as the besiegers to get possession.
And if the besieged are aware of the enemies design, they
may stop the entrance on their side, by which it will be
impossible for them to make use of them against the
place. It is true that the besieged deprive themselves
of the use of the rest of their countermines, unless they
are loaded and stopped beforehand, which is not to be
done in certain circumstances.

If these stratagems should be foreseen by the besieged
and prevented mostly, yet by means of the globe of
compression, their galleries may be destroyed so as to be
quite useless, the besieged will be enabled to proceed in
their trenches, and raise their batteries without any other
disturbance but from above-ground. From whence
it clearly appears, that the countermines, formerly the
greatest obstacle of a siege, are now of very little advantage to a fortified place.

The great effect of powder, though not confined, as
hitherto thought necessary, has been known long
ago. In the duke of Sully's memoirs, page 136,
octavo edit. vol. I. we find this remarkable passage;
" the king of Navarre took Monsegur. Captain Milon
" inclosed five hundred pounds of powder in a bag,
" which he found means to introduce into a drain, from
" the town into the ditch between two principal gates
" of the town; the end of the leader was hid in the grass.
" Every thing being ready to play off this machine,
" the king gave us leave to go and see its effect; which
" was surprising. For one of the gates was thrown
" into the middle of the town, and the other into the

N   " field,

" field, fifty paces from the wall: all the vaults were
" deftroyed, and a paffage was made in the wall for
" 3 men to enter a-breaft, by which the town was
" taken."

M. Valliere's Differtation on Mines, and their Advantages in the Defence of Places.

I fhall not give, in this differtation, the conftruction of mines or countermines, the pofition of liftners, chambers, their charges, nor the manner of ufing them; but only a general idea of the advantages which may be drawn from countermines, if they were conftructed and defended as they fhould be. To explain every thing, it would be neceffary to enter into the particulars of the practice, befides trigonometry; treat of the theory of the collifion of bodies; the communication of motion; the refiftance of folids on the various forces of percuffion, and elafticity of the flame, arifing from different quantities of powder on the time; the different manner of its inflammation, in different fire-arms, according as the fire is conveyed; and, in fhort, into the phyfico-mathematical knowledge, which requires a chain of demonftrations fufficient to fill a large volume, of which this difcourfe could only ferve as a preface.

When Spain made the conqueft of the kingdom of Naples from the French, Francis George, an Italian architect at Naples, propofed to Peter Navarre, the Spanifh general, befieging at that time the caftle del Ovo, a method of becoming foon mafter of this caftle; the French who defended it, were the firft who felt the effect of powder in mines; the architect, whether by knowledge or by chance, placing the powder in fuch a manner, that he threw the wall and garrifon into the fea. This was then the origin of the artificial vulcano, invented to facilitate the taking of places; but it is found on the contrary, that it is more advantageous in the defence, without having as yet been rightly confidered.

It

It is known, that the perfection of arts and sciences is reserved to succeeding generations. With respect to the science of mines, judging from what has been practised, there are certain principles, which, according to all appearances, have not as yet been discovered; and from which are deduced such facts and advantageous means for the defence of places, as would be unpardonable in us to have neglected.

What I have seen best on the effect and construction of mines, are memoirs, containing several experiments of mines made since these twenty-five years; giving the charges of mines pretty exactly, and the diameters of the excavations, according to their different lines of least resistance; I say pretty exactly, because there is a certain rule and geometrical accuracy to be observed in these things, not mentioned in those memoirs. For instance, it has been found in practice,* that a less quantity of powder is required, in proportion to the earth, in large mines than in small: the reason given by some is, that a great quantity of powder produces a greater force in proportion than a less: but those that argue in this manner would soon have discovered their error, had they considered, that not only the weight to be raised is to be considered, but likewise the tenacity of the parts; and as the tenacities are proportional to the surfaces, and the weights to the solid formed by the excavation; and the surfaces of large bodies are less in proportion than in small; the charges of large mines should be less in proportion than those in small.

This discourse on the proportion of charges only, shews the necessity of geometry in the use of mines; the bare knowledge of the practice is not sufficient to understand what has here been said: there are besides other cases, wherein it rarely succeeds, though it be sufficient in the

N 2 attack

---

* All the subsequent argument appears to be without foundation, by all the experiments made at la Fere at different times. For it was found that the charges were always proportional to the quantities of earth blown up, or the globe of compression. M. Valliere has not lessened the charges of large mines in his tables; which also contradict what is here said.

attack of a place not countermined; becaufe when no-thing obftructs the miners paffage, it is eafy to blow up a counterfcarp and make a breach in a baftion, and if fome mines do not fucceed, it is owing to the ignorance, fcarcely pardonable, of thofe who undertake to conftruct them, unlefs fome unforefeen heterogeneous matter in-tervenes, and forces the powder to act differently from what it would have done in an uniform foil; but this accident happens oftner through ignorance than any thing elfe, becaufe a fkilful miner commonly knows where thefe inconveniences are to be apprehended, and if he does not know how to remedy them, he fhould at leaft give notice to the general.

It has not yet been rightly diftinguifhed, how far the word Countermine agrees to mines prepared for the de-fence of places; all know how much they intimidate the befiegers, but the harm they have hitherto done is nothing in comparifon to what they may do, and what obftruction they may make. I fhall not pretend to fay, that they may render a place abfolutely impregnable, but I do not fee how, with equal fkill, to overcome all the obftacles, nor to fucceed in an attack of a place countermined properly, and fkilfully defended.

It is prefuppofed that I mean the fituation of a place proper for mines, well fortified, with a fufficient gar-rifon to defend it, provided with warlike ftores, provi-fions, and every thing elfe, which experience has fhewn to be neceffary.

A miner that knows how to ufe countermines con-ftructed as they fhould be, may ftop the enemy's miners, ftifle them, or deftroy their works in fuch a manner, as to make it impoffible for others to return to the fame place, or, if he pleafe, let them enter the galleries, block up the paffage, and take them prifoners, or kill them if thought proper. In fhort, the befieged who know how to take all advantages, will be mafter of the fate of their enemies: for without mentioning all the traps and ftra-tagems which the enemies cannot forefee; finding it impoffible

poffible to advance, and the under-ground paffages being
ftopped, and not being able to make mines that can be
of any ufe to them; if neceffity obliges him to brave the
mines, and to carry on the attack above-ground, he muft
be very obftinate to perfift in fpite of all the hardfhips
that the befieged can make him endure, not only in making his approaches, but likewife in making his lodgment on the covert way, and every where elfe, where
he dares to carry on this work.

If he proceeds by fap to the covert-way, it will be
proper to give him notice from time to time, by fome
mines, of the danger he is in; if he makes his attack
fword in hand, mines appear then ufelefs; yet they may
ftartle the troops during the attack, and bury fome men;
but as the excavations may ferve for lodgments, it will
be better to referve the mines for difturbing the work,
and confequently to gain time; befides, thefe firft mines
fhould not be loaded till they are to be ufed, in order
to be always ready to prevent the enemy from advancing,
which cannot be done, if they are charged before. The
enemy being arrived to the covert-way, may attempt to
re-enter the ground, whilft he compleats his lodgment;
but he will again be obftructed, and find on all fides
the fame difficulties as before. So foon as he begins to
raife batteries for making a breach, it will be proper to
deftroy all the lodgments on the covert-way by the uppermoft mines, for very good reafons, and not wait till
the cannons are mounted; for thefe fmall mines loofen
the earth where the cannon are to be, by which the
next mines will throw the cannon, when mounted, towards the town. Thefe batteries being repaired, and
the cannon mounted, which cannot be done in a fhort
time, the mines, which I fuppofe properly difpofed and
charged, will throw the cannon, a fecond time, into the
ditch of the place. Such an adventure muft aftonifh an
enemy, for here is another battery and lodgment to be
made; and when other mines throw the cannon again
into the ditch a third time, if he is bold enough to
venture raifing batteries again, he will meet with the
fame reception. In fhort, when there is a depth of earth

N 3 -of

of 25 or 30 feet, it is eafy to blow up the fame furface near the covert-way, 6 or 7 times, which certainly is more than fufficient to difhearten the moft obftinate enemy.

Thefe mines fhould be difpofed in fuch a manner as not to damage the parapet of the covert-way, that it may remain in a condition to be occupied as oft as the lodgment is demolifhed; at the fame time the faps, communications, and parallels, by which the enemy maintains his lodgment on the covert way, muft not be fpared, fome mines muft continually be fprung, with the precaution to deftroy always thofe works which are found moft complete.

It muft here be obferved, that if the depth of earth near the covert-way admits of being blown up 6 or 7 times, it is eafy on a level ground of that depth to dif-pofe the chambers of mines in fuch a manner, as to blow up the fame fpot 20 times all over the glacis and beyond it, becaufe they are not confined on one fide, as thofe near the covert way.

If the mines made it impracticable to make a breach with cannons, and yet the enemy is obftinately bent to purfue his enterprize, what meafures can he take? Will he have recourfe to efcalades? This fcheme is chimerical, and little to be feared, for a garrifon that knows how to defend itfelf. I mention this, becaufe I happened to be at Landau when befieged in 1704, where the gar-rifon, brave as it was, having done all that could be expected, were at laft in fear of an efcalade; on which fufpicion, they determined, after 2 days debate, unfea-fonably to let the water into the ditch. Will the enemy have recourfe again to mines? There are but two ways to arrive at the place or outwork; the one, to pafs under the ditch from the covert-way; a tedious work, in which he certainly will be obftructed; the other, to throw the counterfcarp into the ditch, and to pafs it by means of an epaulement. In both ways he may fuf-ficiently be obftructed, to be difheartened. But fuppofe he arrives to the body of the work, a principal gallery

with

with liftners, placed behind the fcarp, will render his fuccefs impoffible.

The prefent practice is, that the enemy advances to the covert-way by means of covert-faps, that is, by underground galleries, leaving only half, or a foot of earth over their heads; then throwing down this head, their lodgments are almoft quite finifhed. Nothing is more eafy than to ftop this work, and to oblige the enemy to proceed in another manner, if thought proper.

From thefe general hints of countermines it appears what may done, when joined to a proper conduct of the garrifon, which may and fhould, by a well-regulated conduct, contribute to the entire deftruction of the enemy, in taking advantage of all the diforders he is put in, by the effects of countermines. It muft be confeffed, that this is the beft, and perhaps the only defence, from which fuch great advantages can be made.

As we have not as yet heard or feen a defence of this nature, what I have faid in favour of countermines, may perhaps appear a mere imagination; yet I advance nothing but what is grounded on theory and confirmed by experience; it is matter of fact, and I not only can affert the poffibility, but likewife the eafinefs of its execution.

No countermines I have feen, in the feveral attacks I have been at, were difpofed in a proper manner, nor all the advantage made of them, if properly exerted. It is true, that thefe advantages depend on fuch mechanical principles as are taught by geometry, which few miners are acquainted with.

I muft own, that 15 or 20 miners commonly fent into a place befieged are by no means fufficient; for the moft that they can do, is to make a few mines here and there under the glacis, which only frightens the enemy without doing any great harm; the little time that is gained by them is not worth mentioning. Befides, for want of communications, the mines muft be charged at the approach of the enemy to the covert-way, which is a great difadvantage; to this I may add, that if the num-

ber

ber of miners were greater, if their works are not begun before the fiege, the fituations are oft fuch, that very little refource can be expected from them.

To prepare fuch countermines as I propofe, requires time and expence, but neither are fo confiderable as might be imagined: in 3 or 4 months, if no rock intervenes, a place may be fufficiently countermined, as far as 60 or 70 fathom from the covert-way, fuppofing a fufficient number of workmen. As to the expence, it is a mere trifle, in comparifon to the many millions of livres the fortification of a place cofts, to preferve which requires all the care and precaution that is poffible; for in a front of a polygon of 200 fathoms, I fuppofe requires 2000 fathoms of galleries, which may perhaps coft 35000 livres in materials and workmanfhip, and 100,000 lb. of powder in referve for that ufe.

It muft be obferved, that if fuch a work be undertaken, it fhould be carried on with all fpeed, and without intermiffion; all the parts of a place, fufceptible of making mines, fhould be finifhed together, for it would be dangerous to be attacked in a front not prepared, whilft all the others are; it will befides inftruct the enemy of your condition, which he always difcovers too foon.

The fcience of countermines has a fuperiority over that of fortification, becaufe the latter is partly arbitrary, whereas the former is determined by the fituation of the works and nature of the foil: another advantage the mines have, no lefs confiderable than the former, is, that the pofition of thefe mines may be fo varied, as to be impoffible for the moft experienced enemy to gain any intelligence of them.

The galleries fupported with wood, are eafier defended, and more commodious to avoid certain accidents, than thofe made of mafonry; but as wood decays, it is more convenient to make thofe galleries, which are to ftand a confiderable time, with mafonry, by obferving however to make the roof flat, inftead of round as they are commonly made, to prevent certain accidents. As to the objections which may be made againft this method of

making

making countermines; the moft material is, that the miners cannot enter thofe galleries filled with fmoke arifing from the fpringing of a former mine, which fuffocates them; but thefe, and other inconveniences, may be avoided, by a particular conftruction of thefe galleries, which purifies the air, and makes it circulate*.

General Conftruction of the feveral Stages of Countermines.

Fig. 18, in the line g H, reprefenting the flope of the glacis, take the line g F, equal to 4, 5, or 6 feet, for the thicknefs of earth to be left to ferve as a parapet to the covert-way: take F z, equal to half the diameter of the excavation, and z O, the perpendicular to F H to the line of leaft refiftance; then the line F L will reprefent the fection of the plane in which the feveral ftages of countermines are placed. In order to find the diftances of the chambers in that plane, take O M, M L, each equal to F O, and the points O, M, L, will reprefent the centers of the chambers: this may be carried on to any depth. This conftruction is evident from M. Belidor's principles, that the charges of mines are proportional to the cubes of the radii or lines O F, M O, L M, of the globe of compreffion.

M. Valliere will have the line M O always equal to the line of leaft refiftance, O z, of the mine next above it; but obferves, that in a foil of an uniform denfity, experience fhews that thefe lines are to be increafed by one third of the line of leaft refiftance; fo that if the
line

* What this particular conftruction of galleries, which M. Valliere mentions here, is, remains as yet a fecret; nor can it be guefs'd at: for if he means that air-holes may be made from diftance to diftance, they may be difcovered from above, and either ftopped, or fome ftinking compofition thrown through them into the galleries, and thereby increafe inftead of diminifhing the danger: or whether, the galleries, by having feveral entrances, and a communication with one another, can be freed by this means from the fulphurous fmoke, foon enough to be entered and defended when required, can, in my opinion, only be known from experience.

line of leaft refiftance O z is 12 feet, O M fhould be 16;
which anfwers our conftruction nearly. He fuppofes
likewife in his conftruction, that the diameter of the
excavation is always double the line of leaft refiftance;
but we have proved, that it may be triple or quadruple
of that line. It is therefore neceffary in this conftruction
to determine the ratio of the lines F z and z O, from the
charge, to determine the plane F L of the feveral ftages
of mines.

Fig. 19. fhews the difpofition of the chambers of the
countermines, in a fection of the glacis parallel to the
covert-way; and how they fhould be placed under each
other.

Explanations of the Figures.

PLATE I.

Fig. 1. Shews the figure of an excavation.
Fig. 2. Shews how the fame battery has been blown up 3 times
by 3 mines C, D, E, placed below each other.
Fig. 3. Shews the plan of the galleries and chambers.
Fig. 4. Profil of the fame mines lengthways of the battery.
Fig. 5. Shews how a battery is blown up once only.
Fig. 6. The plan of the galleries of the preceding mines.
Fig. 7. Plan of mines conftructed at Bify, to fhew the effect
of the globe of compreffion.
E. Chamber, whofe line of leaft refiftance was 12 feet, and
loaded with 3000 lb. of powder.
I F. Gallery 69 feet long, going from the bottom of the pit I,
and paffing 14 feet under the chamber E.
H G. Branch from the gallery, 14 feet lower, and 8 diftant
from the chamber E.
Fig. 8. Section thro' B A, paffing thro' the chamber E.
YZX. The gallery going from the pit I, floping 18 inches
from Y to Z, the reft being level.
V. T. Horizontal line, and O N the flope of the ground of
5 feet from the gallery A to the gallery B.
R S. A perpendicular of 26 feet.
Fig. 9. Section thro' D C of the plan paffing likewife thro'
the chamber E, and the galleries D, C.

PLATE

P L A T E   II.

Fig. 10. 11. Shewing the extent of the excavation made by the chamber E, fig. 7, and the parts burft of the high and low galleries.

Fig. 12.   The plan of a place of arms D in a covert-way, countermined.

Fig. 13. The fame place of arms, as appeared when the galleries were blown up, to make trenches.

Fig. 14.   The fame as the two former, only cleared and traverfed, to prevent being enfiladed.

Fig. { 15. } A fection of the 13th figure.
     { 16. } A fection through the 14th figure, formed into steps.

P L A T E   III.

Fig. 17. Shews the plan of an attack of a place countermined. The great circles, I, reprefent the effects of the globes of compreffion ; and the little circles the countermines fprung by the befieged to blow up the advanced faps of the befiegers.

F I N I S.

A Scheme to improve Artillery,

For Sea and Land Service.

THE indifpenfable neceffity of having a very large Artillery, for Sea and Land Service, and the extraordinary expence attending it, induces me to hope that this propofal for reducing the weight and expences, may be acceptable; efpecially as no nation have as yet made any fuch attempt.

This is to be confidered under two heads : the one to diminifh the weights; and the other not to ufe any brafs field artillery, but only iron; to leffen the great burthen of our fhips of war, and to carry larger calibers than thofe of other nations of the fame rate. If the weights of our guns are diminifhed, they will require fewer hands to manage them, and of confequence, a fmaller number will be expofed to danger at a time : and if we carry larger calibers, our rates will be a match for larger fhips.

The advantage of ufing iron guns in the field inftead of brafs, will be that the expences are leffened in proportion to the coft of brafs to that of iron, which is as 8 to 1.

The only objection againft iron is, its pretended brittlenefs : but as we abound in iron, that is ftronger and tougher than any brafs, this objection is invalid. This I can affert : having feen fome that cannot be broke by any force, and will flatten like hammer'd iron: if then we ufe fuch iron, there can be no danger of the guns burfting in the moft fevere action.

Though brafs guns are not liable to burft, yet they are fooner rendered unferviceable in action than iron. For by the foftnefs of the metal, the vent widens fo foon, and they are liable to bend at the muzzle, that it would be dangerous to fire them; as we have found by experience at Belleifle, and where we have been obliged to take guns from the fhips to finifh the fiege.

Thefe being undeniable facts, no poffible reafon can be affigned againft ufing iron guns in both fea and land fervice, and thereby leffen the expences of artillery, fo confiderably as will appear by the following tables:

Length

Length and Weights of Iron Ship Guns.

OLD PIECES.			NEW PIECES.		
Calib.	Length	Weight	Calib.	Length	Weigh
	Ft. In.			Ft. In.	
3	4 6	7 1 7	3	3 6	3 3 0
4	6 0	12 2 13	6	4 4	7 2 0
6	7 0	17 1 14	9	5 0	11 1 0
9	7 0	23 2 2	12	5 6	15 0 0
12	9 0	32 3 3	18	6 4	22 2 0
18	9 0	41 1 8	24	7 0	30 0 0
24	9 0	48 0 0	32	7 6	40 0 0
32	9 6	53 3 23	42	8 4	52 2 0
42	10 0	55 1 12	48	8 6	60 0 0

Guns of this conftruction appear fufficiently ftrong from the proof of two three-pounders, made for Lord Egmont, and that they may even be made lighter and of equal fervice.

Length and Weight of Battering Pieces.

OLD BRASS.			NEW IRON.		
Calib.	Length	Weight.	Calib.	Length	Weight.
	Ft. In.			Ft In .	
6	8 0	19 0 0	6	6 1	9 1 0
9	9 0	25 0 0	9	7 0	14 0 0
12	9 0	29 0 0	12	7 8	18 0 0
18	9 6	48 0 0	18	9 0	29 1 0
24	9 6	51 0 0	24	9 8	37 3 0
32	10 0	55 2 0	32	9	42 0 0

Total 227

Total 151 0
Diff. 76 2 0

That

That thefe guns are fufficiently ftrong, is evident from the former trial; befides, there are feveral 32 pounders of the fame dimenfions and weight now exifting and ferviceable, though caft in King Charles the Second's time.

N. B. Thefe battering pieces may ferve in Garrifons.

It appears from thefe tables that no proportion has beeen obferved in any guns hitherto made, in refpect to their length or weight, but merely by guefs.

Some examples to fhew what may be faved by this fcheme.

The Royal George carries a hundred brafs guns, which weigh together 218.2 tons, the ton coft 130 pounds, workmanfhip included.

The expence of thefe guns is then - - 28366 pounds

A fet of the iron guns of the fame number and calibers, according to my conftruction, weighs } 127.8 tons

The ton coft 16 pounds, and the whole fet } 2044.8 pounds

The Royal George carries then 90.4 tons more than is neceffary, and the difference between the expence is } 26321.2 pounds

That is 12.5 times more than the new iron fet cofts: or twelve fhips of the fame rate may be fitted out lefs charge.

A fet of the { Old } irons guns for a { 204.4 } tons
               { New } firft-rate weighs { 127.8 }

The difference betwen the weights of the old and new is } 76.6 tons

The difference between the expence is then } 1225.6 pounds

A fet of brafs battering pieces weighs   11.36 tons
A ton coft 130 pounds, and the fet   1476.8 pounds
A fet of the new weighs - - - - -   7.55 tons
The ton cofts 16 pounds, and the fet   117.8 pounds

That is 11 times, and 632 over, more than the new fet, or eleven fets of the new, could be made at lefs expence than one of the old.

The

This table shews what may be saved in the Navy; and if we add those on board sloops, the different garrisons, and the field train, with the great expence of their carriage in the field, it may be found pretty near as much more.

Numb. of Guns.	Weight of Old.		Weight of New.		Differ.		No. of Ships.	Total Difference	
100	4367	3	2556	0	1811	3	5	9058	0
90	3537	3	2001	0	1536	3	9	13827	3
80	3108	3	1827	0	1287	3	7	9014	1
74	3091	0	1840	2	1250	2	32	40016	0
70	2997	0	1796	2	1200	2	10	12005	0
64	2543	3	1305	0	1238	2	23	28485	2
60	2177	3	1185	0	972	3	30	29782	2
50	1881	1	1035	0	846	1	19	16078	3
44	1365	2	705	0	660	2	8	5284	0
40	1234	2	312	2	922	0	9	8298	0
36	963	3	450	0	513	3	7	3596	1
32	956	2	435	0	521	2	28	14602	0
28	593	2	285	0	308	2	23	7095	1
24	531	3	255	0	276	3	12	3321	0
20	421	2	191	1	230	1	15	3453	3

Difference between the Weights - - - - - 203918　3　0

Expences of the { Brass guns of two first rates, —— 203918　15　0
Iron ditto　—— —— —— 53109　5　0

We get　£. 257028　0　0

If then no material objection can be made to this proposal, so beneficial to the nation, I humbly hope that it will be put in practice, and that my trouble of composing it, after above fifty years application, to theory and practice, will be considered.

JOHN MULLER.

Proportion of Ammunition for the following Troops, being the Extra Allowance for one Year, commencing the 25th of March, agreeable to King's Warrant, 1760.

	Powder. Barrels.	Ball. Musqt. C.	Ball. Carbine. C.	Ball. Pistol. C.	Flints. Musqt. No.	Flints. Carbine. No.	Flints. Pistol. No.
A Regiment of Foot of 900 Men for - { Service	13½	35			2700		
{ Exercife	19	11			1800		
A Regiment of Dragoons of 360 Men for { Service	5	9		2	1134		2268
{ Exercife	7	1			756		1512
A Light Troop of 121 Men for - - - { Service	2½		7			363	393
{ Exercife	1⅛					242	262

N. B. The

N. B. The proportion of ammunition for a regiment of foot is 64 rounds for each man for fervice, at 6 drachms each cartridge, and 135 rounds each man for exercife, at $\frac{1}{4}$ of an oz.

Mufquet flints, 3 to each man for fervice, and 2 for exercife.

Mufquet balls, 20 to each man for exercife.

The proportion for a regiment of dragoons is one pound of powder for fervice, and two pounds for exercife to each man ; each cartridge to contain the fame as thofe of the foot.

The proportion for the light dragoons is 64 rounds for each man for fervice, at $\frac{1}{4}$ of an oz. each cartridge, and 405 rounds each man for exercife, at 3 drachms each cartridge.

The battalions of militia embodied are to have the fame proportion of ammunition as a regiment of foot, according to their numbers.

Office of Ordnance, May 14, 1760.

Form of a Certificate for Ammunition to be addreffed to the Right Hon. and Hon. the BOARD OF ORDNANCE, whenever a Supply of Ammunition is wanted.

THESE are to certify the Right Honourable and Honourable the BOARD OF ORDNANCE, that the laft Supply of Ammunition received for Ufe of Regiment of   or Company of under the Command of   is nearly expended in the Duty and Exercife of the faid   Witnefs my Hand this   Day of

To the Rt. Hon. and Hon. the Board of Ordnance.

F I N I S.

Printed for and Sold by J. MILLAN.

1 COLDBATCH on Mifletoe, 1s.
2 Bradley's Survey of Hufbandry, 4s.
3 Bradley's Lectures, 3s.
4 Barrow's Medicinal Dictionary, 8s.
5 Sydenham's Compendium Medicinae.
6 All Shell and other Fifh, both Salt and Frefh Water, brought to
    Market, with the Times of their being in Seafon, from the
    original Paintings of VANHAEKEN, engraved on 9 full Sheet
    Copper Plates, 10s. 6d.———1l. 1l. coloured.
7 Hill's Review of the Royal Society, 4to. 10s. 6d.
8 Palladio, finely engraved by Ware, 7s. 6d.
9 Langley's Gothic Architecture, 4to. 15s.
10 Inigo Jones's Defigns for Cielings, Chimneys, Temples, &c.
    10s. 6d.
12 Morris's Lectures on Architecture, 2 Parts, 6s.
13 Price's Carpentry, 4to. 7s. 6d.
14 Antiquities of Hereford Cathedral, 8vo.
15 Perrault's Architecture, Folio, 10s. 6d.
16 Pozzo's Perspective, Folio, 15s.
17 Caftell's Villas of the Ancients, Folio.
18 Newton's Fluxions, 8vo.
19 Mead on Poifons, 8vo.
20 Orthopœdia, or the Art of correcting and preventing Defor-
    mities in Children, 2 vol. Cuts.
21 Dr. Sharpe's Englifh-Hebrew and Englifh-Latin Grammar.
22 Dr. Sharpe's Defence of Chriftianity, 2 Parts, 6s. Oligarchy 1s.
23 Tandon's French Grammar to learn without a Mafter, 2s.
24 Pine's Horace, 2 vol. 2l. 2s.
25 Maafvicii Virgilius, 2 tom. 12mo. 2l. 6s.
26 Nollet's Compendium of the Bible, Fr. and Eng. 2 v. 12mo. 6s.
28 Letters from a Perfian in England, 3s.
29 Prior's Pofthumous Works, 2 vol. 8vo. 12s.
30 Prior's Poems, 12mo. vol. ii. 3s.
31 Buckingham's Works, 2 vol. 8vo.
32 Vane's Letters.
33 Ozell's Telemachus, 2 vol. 8vo. 10s.
34 Atkins's Tracts, 8vo. 5s.
35 Malcolm's Tracts, 8vo. 5s.
36 Howell's Letters, 8vo. 5s.
37 Haywood's Love Letters, 4s.
38 Haywood's Cleomelia, 1s. 6d.
39 Pope's Works, vol. i. 4to. large Paper, 10s.
40 Love and Friendfhip, a Comedy, 1s. 6d.
41 Petty's Political Arithmetick, 3s. 6d.
42 Petty's Effays, 3s.
43 War of the Beafts, 3s.
44 Cambridge's Account of the War in India, 4to. 15s.
45 ——————————————8vo. 6s.
46 Ducarel's Anglo-Norman Antiquities, Folio, 1l. 1s.
47 Ducarel's Anglo-Gallic Coins, 4to. 10s. 6d.
48 Hiftory of the Severambians, 8vo. 2s.
49 Cox's Hiftory of Carolana, 8vo.

Made in the USA
Las Vegas, NV
13 July 2023

74701719R00116